The Effective DRE:
A Theology Series

Means of Grace, Ways of Life: Sacramental Theology

BY KURT STASIAK, O.S.B.

TOM WALTERS
SERIES EDITOR

NATIONAL CONFERENCE FOR
CATECHETICAL LEADERSHIP

Loyola Press

NATIONAL CONFERENCE FOR CATECHETICAL LEADERSHIP

3021 Fourth Street, N.E.
Washington, D.C. 20017-1102
1-202-636-3826

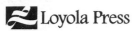 Loyola Press

3441 North Ashland Avenue
Chicago, Illinois 60657
1-800-621-1008

Nihil Obstat: Rev. Daniel J. Mahan, S.T.B., S.T.L.
　　　　　　Censor Librorum

Imprimatur: Rev. Msgr. Joseph F. Schaedel
　　　　　　Vicar General/Moderator of the Curia

Given at Indianapolis, Indiana, on December 21, 1999
Feast of St. Peter Canisius

The *nihil obstat* and *imprimatur* are official declarations that a book is free of doctrinal and moral error. No implication is contained herein that those who have granted the nihil obstat and imprimatur agree with the content, opinions, or statements expressed.

Acknowledgments:
An earlier version of some of the material presented in Chapter 5 and in Appendix II originally appeared as "Infant Baptism Reclaimed: Forgotten Truths about Infant Baptism" in *The Living Light: Liturgy and Catechesis*. Volume 31, no. 3 (Spring 1995). Copyright © 1995 United States Catholic Conference, Inc., Washington, D.C. Used with permission. All rights reserved.

An earlier version of some of the material presented in Chapter 6 originally appeared as "Of Sacraments and Sacrifice" in *Assembly*, Volume 23, no.6 (November 1997). Copyright © 1997 Notre Dame Center for Pastoral Liturgy. Notre Dame, IN. Used with permission. All rights reserved.

Acknowledgments continued on p. 160

ISBN: 0-8294-1494-0

00　01　02　03　04　5　4　3　2　1　　　　　Printed in Canada

Table of Contents

About This Series

The **Effective DRE: A Theology Series** has been developed by the National Conference for Catechetical Leadership (NCCL) to provide directors of religious education (DREs) and those preparing to become DREs with an introductory and orderly understanding and interpretation of the truths of revelation. As in the earlier series, **The Effective DRE: A Skills Development Series**, we use the term DRE as broadly as possible and intend it to refer to anyone involved in or planning to become involved in a leadership capacity in a parish religious education program. And, also like the earlier series, these booklets, though addressed specifically to DREs, can be of assistance to all parish catechetical leaders, regardless of their title or the scope of their job description.

Each booklet was written to assist DREs in meeting the theological requirements specified in the *National Certification Standards for Professional Parish Directors of Religious Education*, a document developed by the NCCL and approved by the United States Catholic Conference Commission on Certification and Accreditation. The series covers the following topics: Scripture, Sacramental Theology, Church History, Ecclesiology, Christology, Morality, Ecumenism, Mary and the Saints, and Theological Reflection.

Each booklet is written with the intent of helping DREs gain access to the Catholic tradition in a way that allows them to apply it to their lives and their catechetical ministry. It is our hope that these booklets will serve not only as a personal resource for self-study but also as a resource in formal diocesan and parish training programs for catechetical leaders/DREs. The reflection questions at the end of each chapter lend themselves not only to personal reflection but group discussion as well.

In addition, the authors have drawn extensively from both the *Catechism of the Catholic Church* and the recently published *General Directory for Catechesis*. This has resulted in a series that is both informative and up-to-date.

Like the earlier series, this series is designed to serve as a resource to DREs in their efforts to foster the growth of faith in those whom they serve.

Tom Walters
Series Editor

Introduction

"A" ctions speak louder than words." This timeworn cliché may seem a strange way to introduce a study on liturgy and the sacraments. Tired as the saying may be, however, its message is true—and is most apt to the subject of this book.

Actions speak louder than words. The sacraments are among the most important ways Catholic Christians practice—among the most important ways we *act out*—what it is we believe. The Catholic faith is a discipline of doctrines and dogmas, a religion of teachings and precepts. Most of all, however, our Catholic faith is a way of life that constantly calls us to put into practice what it is we profess in our creed. What we as Catholics believe in our minds is supposed to guide how we act in the world.

Actions speak louder than words. The late German theologian, Hans Urs von Balthasar, once offered the religious equivalent of this cliché. He suggested that it is not so important that the value of Christianity be seen in itself, but that it is absolutely crucial that Christianity's value be seen *in us*. In other words, if the world wants to know what we believe as Christians, it should be able to learn that simply by observing us as we go about the ordinary business of our lives. Ultimately, the most effective homilies on the Gospels are not those given by the priest in church, but by those Christians who preach day in and day out by living in the world what they, in church, say they believe.

Actions speak louder than words. For us Catholics, the liturgy and the sacraments are actions that speak particularly loud and clear. The sacraments are *visible words*, as Saint Augustine wrote in the fifth century: they are words we can see and touch, words we can act out—words we must act upon. The sacraments are not rituals we perform when we go to church. Rather, they are sacred actions that we do because we *are* Church. And what we do in a church building misses the mark if it does not influence— orient, guide, challenge, and support—what we do with our lives in the world.

THE GOAL AND FOCUS OF THIS BOOKLET

This booklet is an introduction to the history, theology, and pastoral practice of the Church's liturgy and her sacraments. It is intended for directors of religious education (DREs), particularly those who have not had the opportunity to engage in a formal, systematic program of theological study and reflection. This booklet provides many facts about the Church's ritual celebrations. More important than presenting facts, however, this booklet tries to help readers better understand how the Church thinks about her sacraments—and why.

The Council of Trent declared that there were seven sacraments, but conceded that not all were of equal value in the work of our salvation. DREs know they will not be devoting equal amounts of their time and resources to each of the seven sacraments. This booklet reflects both these "inequalities." The primary emphasis is on the liturgy and the sacraments in general: those thoughts and principles that apply to the Church's whole sacramental economy. Baptism and Eucharist, the two preeminent sacramental actions of our Church, each merit a separate chapter. The remaining five sacraments are dealt with according to the professional involvement DREs ordinarily have or can expect to have with them.

NATIONAL CERTIFICATION STANDARDS

The liturgy and the sacraments lie at the heart of the Church's identity, life, and mission. To study them, therefore, is to study the Scriptures, Church history and dogma, Christology, and other numerous theological disciplines. This booklet, concerned primarily with the liturgy and the sacraments, touches many theological fields and so, at least indirectly, addresses a number of the *National Certification Standards for Professional Parish Directors of Religious Education* (*Standards*). Special attention is given to the following "Theological Standards":

• An understanding of "Catholic doctrine and belief as presented in the documents of Vatican Council II, the *Catechism of the Catholic Church*, and other relevant Church documents," and so the ability to "teach persons the foundations of Catholic faith and doctrine, as well as the current teachings of the Church" (*Standards*, #520.03).

• An understanding of "the Church's historical and traditional development and its relevance to the modern Church," and so the ability to "explain the Church's heritage and communicate the teachings of the magisterium" (*Standards*, #520.04).

• An understanding of "the theological and historical development of the Eucharist, sacramental, liturgical, and devotional life of the Church," and so the ability to "prepare creative, spirit-filled liturgies, sacramental celebrations and prayer experiences" (*Standards*, #520.13).

• An understanding of "the uniqueness of the Catholic faith tradition in relation to other Christian traditions," and so the ability to "help members of the parish community articulate Catholic beliefs and practices, especially the key elements of the Catholic faith" (*Standards*, #520.17).

Concerning the "Professional Standards" set forth by the *Standards*, this booklet pays particular attention to:

• An understanding of "the history and essential principles of the Church's liturgical and sacramental life as found in the appropriate documentary tradition of the universal, national, and local Church," and so the ability to "explain the history and meaning of the liturgy and sacramental rites of our Church to catechists, parents, and adult learners" (*Standards*, #532.301).

• An understanding of "current liturgical principles and the revised rites of the Church," and so the ability to "use current liturgical principles in designing and leading learning sessions for adults, adolescents, and children for the immediate preparation for the sacraments of Eucharist, reconciliation, and confirmation" (*Standards*, #532.302).

• An understanding of "the Eucharist as the source and summit of the Christian life," and so the ability to "explain the meaning and structure of the Mass to catechists, parents, and adult learners" (*Standards*, #532.303).

THE STRUCTURE OF THIS BOOKLET

As mentioned, the primary emphasis of this booklet is on the liturgy and the sacraments in general. Chapter 1 discusses two fundamental principles of the liturgy and the sacraments: that the liturgy understood is the work of the Church and of God. The following three chapters delve into some of the more important Church teachings on the sacraments, using the traditional definition of the sacraments as "visible signs instituted by Christ to give grace" as a guide.

Chapter 2 examines the sacraments as visible signs, and Chapter 3 explores what the Church teaches about the sacraments conferring the gift of grace. Chapter 4 discusses the institution of the sacraments by Christ, offers a brief history of the early development of each of the seven sacraments, and provides an overview of how the Church has thought about and approached the sacraments throughout her history.

Chapter 5 deals with Baptism, the first sacrament Christians celebrate—indeed, the sacramental action of the Church that makes us Christian and Catholic. Both adult and infant Baptism are discussed: these two expressions of the one sacrament are unique enough that they deserve a separate, though certainly related, consideration. DREs may or may not be concerned with preparing parents for the Baptism of their children, but they are often involved in the Rite of Christian Initiation of Adults (RCIA), the Rite of Christian Initiation of Children (RCIC), and in preparing children and young adults for the sacraments of Reconciliation and Confirmation. Since Baptism is our "first sacrament," a better understanding of it can only enhance our understanding and appreciation of the sacraments we subsequently receive.

Chapter 6 outlines the history and theology of the Eucharist, what *Lumen Gentium (LG)*, the Second Vatican Council's *Dogmatic Constitution on the Church*, has described as "the source and summit of the Christian life" (#11). Chapter 7 offers a brief discussion of the remaining five sacraments of our Church, with special emphasis— theological and pastoral—on the sacraments of Reconciliation and Confirmation, two sacraments with which DREs are often involved as regards their planning and preparation.

HOW TO USE THIS BOOKLET

This booklet does not stand by itself, and should not be thought of as an exhaustive study of either the history or theology of the liturgy and the sacraments. It is an introduction to the study of the sacraments—a first book, a primer—for those committed to further study and reflection. As such, appropriate and necessary companions to this booklet include resources such as the *Catechism of the Catholic Church* (*CCC*) and the documents of the Second Vatican Council. The reader is encouraged to delve into other works that address the history and theology of the sacraments in greater depth. (One example is Joseph Martos's *Doors to the Sacred: A Historical Introduction to Sacraments in the Catholic Church*, referred to in our text and cited in the Bibliography.)

I have incorporated several features into this booklet in an effort to make it as helpful and reader-friendly as possible. Each chapter, for example, begins with the listing of several "Key Questions" designed to provide a preview of what lies ahead, and to help readers focus their attention on the more important points that will be discussed. Following these opening questions are several points under the heading "As We Begin." These are short statements of fact—often historical notes—that quickly give readers background information pertaining to the discussion that follows. A "Chapter Summary" and questions "For Reflection" conclude each chapter, assisting readers in mastering and, more importantly, applying the sacramental concepts and principles that have been discussed.

Appendix I provides a wealth of useful information in the form of three charts. Appendix II supplements our discussion of the sacrament of Baptism in Chapter 4, by offering a short essay on a particular theological model for understanding the significance of that sacrament.

Finally, while we need know neither technical language nor Latin to celebrate the sacraments worthily, as is the case with any field, sacramental theology has its own expressions, definitions, and heroes. A Glossary offers additional information about the more important concepts and people.

Actions speak louder than words. And the value of Christianity, ultimately, must be seen in us. The sacraments are *visible words* that lead us to the treasures of our life in Christ. That these treasures are sometimes subtle, sometimes ordinary—even sometimes hidden—does not belie their importance to our lives as individual Christians and to the life of our Church. The ultimate aim of this booklet is to suggest the value of these treasures, and to provide some tools to locate and unearth them.

I dedicate this booklet to my parents, Joe and Suzanne. They were my first teachers in the faith, my first "directors of religious education." And, because actions do speak louder than words, they were often the best.

Abbreviations

CCC   *Catechism of the Catholic Church*

SC   *Sacrosanctum Concilium (The Constitution on the Sacred Liturgy)*

DRE   Director of Religious Education

LG   *Lumen Gentium (The Dogmatic Constitution on the Church)*

RBC   Rite of Baptism for Children

RCIA   Rite of Christian Initiation of Adults

RCIC   Rite of Christian Initiation of Children

Standards   *National Certification Standards for Professional Parish Directors of Religious Education*

1 Liturgy: Some First Thoughts

KEY QUESTIONS

• What is liturgy?

• Why is it important for the Church to have a liturgy?

• What is the purpose of liturgy?

• Who is involved in the Church's liturgy?

AS WE BEGIN

• Pope John XXIII announced his intention to convene the Second Vatican Council in January 1959. In his words, the Council was to be a *pastoral* one: a council that was less intent on defining new doctrines or presenting new teachings, and more attentive to explaining how Catholics were to live out their faith in today's world. The first of the Council's four sessions began in October 1962. Vatican Council II officially concluded on December 8, 1965.

• Published on December 4, 1963, *Sacrosanctum Concilium* (*SC*), the *Constitution on the Sacred Liturgy,* was the first document promulgated by the Council. That this document was published first shows how important the Council considered the liturgy to be to the pastoral life of the Church. The opening paragraph reflects this conviction: "The sacred Council has set out to impart an ever-increasing vigor to the Christian life of the faithful . . . Accord-

1

ingly it sees particularly cogent reasons for undertaking the reform and promotion of the liturgy" (#1).

An oft-cited passage from *SC* is that the liturgy "is the summit toward which the activity of the Church is directed [and] it is also the fount from which all her power flows" (#10). Earlier in this *Constitution*, we find a succinct explanation of why this is so:

> For it is the liturgy through which, especially in the divine sacrifice of the Eucharist, 'the work of our redemption is accomplished,' and it is through the liturgy, especially, that the faithful are enabled to express in their lives and manifest to others the mystery of Christ and the real nature of the true Church. (*SC*, #2)

Clearly, the liturgy is of the utmost importance! It accomplishes the work of our redemption. It enables us to witness to others who we are because of what Christ has done for us. The liturgy does something *in* us, *for* us, *to* us, so that we may do something *in*, *for*, and *to* the world. The liturgy is of the utmost importance indeed! But what, exactly, does the word *liturgy* mean?

LITURGY IS THE WORK OF THE PEOPLE

The word *liturgy* comes from the Greek words for "people" and "work." As is the case with many religious or theological words we use today, *liturgy* originally had a secular or political meaning; it referred to a public work, such as a building project. *Liturgy* was also a work undertaken by the state to benefit its people, such as the establishment and maintenance of an educational system.

These originally secular meanings of the word *liturgy* shed light on our use of the word today. In fact, understanding our Catholic liturgy as a "public work done to benefit people" is not only appropriate, but it can help us understand what we mean by liturgy—and why we do liturgy—in an entirely new light. Let us consider what we mean when we say liturgy is "the work of the people."

Liturgy Is Work

Ordinarily, we don't think of liturgy as *work* and, unfortunately, too many times for too many people, liturgy is anything *but* work. Liturgy is *sitting* in church or *listening* to a homily; liturgy is *receiving* a sacrament or *being blessed* by a priest. But liturgy as *work*?

My old *American Heritage Dictionary of the English Language* defines *work* as "physical or mental effort or activity directed toward the production or accomplishment of something." A second definition states that work is "employment, a job." These are secular definitions, but they suggest something important about the "holy work," the "holy employment," our liturgy is—and that our liturgy demands of us.

Liturgy is work; it is something we do. Liturgy is an activity, an exercise that requires effort, not mere observation. Why do we celebrate liturgy? What is the *work* of liturgy? We celebrate the liturgy because we believe certain things about God, our Church, and ourselves—and we celebrate the liturgy because we want to make those beliefs known. To speak of the Church *celebrating* liturgy is to speak of the Church putting into practice what she professes to believe. The work of liturgy is our participating in the work of God. As the *CCC* says:

> Through the liturgy Christ, our redeemer and high priest, continues the work of our redemption in, with, and through his Church. (#1069)

Our liturgy is work because it is our employment, our job—or, to use religious vocabulary, the liturgy is our *vocation*, our *calling*. Secularly, we seek employment in order to live. We hold a job not just to clean the streets or keep budgets in order or supply groceries to those around us. Rather, we work to get our lives in order, to bring in more money than we are obliged to give away, and to put food on our table. We work, in other words, so that we can support ourselves and live the best life we can.

Similarly, the work of liturgy is not just to "get things done": to gather a congregation, to sing hymns, to collect money, to encourage fellowship. These things, of course, are part of the work of liturgy. But the primary reason we do the work of liturgy is to get our lives in order, to receive all that God has to offer so that we will have more than enough to give to others, and to nourish ourselves through the love and grace of God that the liturgy makes manifest to us. We do the work of liturgy because we are the Church, and the liturgy is the primary means by which our Church supports, defines, and guides herself spiritually and pastorally. Recall the words of *SC*:

> The liturgy is the summit toward which the activity of the Church is directed; it is also the fount from which all her power flows. (#10)

The liturgy is the Church's employment, her job. The liturgy is the Church's vocation and calling. We celebrate liturgy because we are Church. *We celebrate liturgy so that we will be Church*.

This does not mean that the only activity the Church is involved in is liturgical celebrations and sacred rituals. Rather, it means that the Church is supported, strengthened, and guided in all her works through her work of the liturgy. In fact, it is the liturgy that gives purpose to all the works of the Church, the two most important of which are the praise of God and our growing in holiness. What is often said of the Eucharist can be applied to the liturgy and to all the sacraments: "The Church makes the liturgy and the sacraments, and the liturgy and the sacraments do make the Church."

LITURGY IS THE WORK OF ALL THE FAITHFUL

The Second Vatican Council clearly distinguished the ministerial, or ordained, priesthood from the priesthood of all the faithful (see *Lumen Gentium* [*LG*] #10). It insisted, however, that all Catholics, by virtue of their Baptism, shared in some way in the priesthood of Christ. Fundamental to the liturgical renewal initiated by the Council is the notion that the liturgy of the Church is the work of the whole Church. *SC* describes the liturgy as "an exercise of the priestly office of Jesus Christ" (#7). Liturgy is not the property or the domain of the clergy, and so the Council insists that:

> All the faithful should be led to that full, conscious, and active participation in liturgical celebrations which is demanded by the very nature of the liturgy, and to which the Christian people, 'a chosen race, a royal priesthood, a holy nation, a redeemed people' (1 Pet. 2:9, 4–5), have a right and obligation by reason of their baptism. (*SC*, #14)

The liturgy can be seen as the work of the people because each congregation shares in Christ's own prayer to his Father (see *CCC*, #1073). Additionally, the liturgy is the work of the people of God as they exercise their share in the priestly office of Christ. The liturgy is the most important work—the most important employment—a Catholic can do. As *SC* reminds us:

> Every liturgical celebration, because it is an action of Christ the Priest and of his Body, which is the Church, is a sacred action surpassing all others. No other action of the Church can equal its efficacy by the same title and to the same degree. (*SC*, #7)

Let us return once more to the notion that liturgy is the work of the people.

LITURGY IS, INDEED, WORK

Liturgy is work; to truly do the work of the liturgy is work! Liturgy is not something that takes place only within the church building. Liturgy is the building of the Church and, as the above citation makes clear, liturgy is the premier action of the Church.

A liturgical celebration may have a clearly defined beginning and end. But, because of its importance in and to the life of the Church, there is much that must come *before* that celebration, just as there is much that must take place *because* of it. The *CCC* reminds us that liturgy:

> . . . must be preceded by evangelization, faith, and conversion. . . . [so that it] can then produce its fruits in the lives of the faithful: new life in the Spirit, involvement in the mission of the Church, and service to her unity. (#1072)

Liturgy is work because it demands preparation, commitment, and action. To understand the true nature and purpose of liturgy, we need to realize that our lives must be different outside of church because of what we do when we are in church. The Gospels are clear: religion—growing in holiness—is not simply about one's relationship with God. When asked what the greatest commandment is, Jesus offers two: "Love God with everything you have and are; love your neighbor as yourself" (see Matthew 22:37–39). Christians do not have the choice of specializing in one love or the other. They must be practitioners of both, for it is concerning both that they will be judged. To be baptized a Christian—that is, to be incorporated into Christ and into his Church—is to set aside forever the notion that the way to salvation is found only in our worship of God. The parable of the last judgment in

Matthew's Gospel (see Chapter 25:31–46) paints a haunting picture of the absolute necessity of recognizing God in our neighbor. Those who are condemned are those who would have given food to the hungry or drink to the thirsty *if only* they had known that they were rending praise to the Lord by tending to those in need.

What is liturgy? Liturgy is the work of the people of God. Liturgy is the people of God putting what they believe into practice. Liturgy is work because it demands "full and active participation": preparation, commitment, and action.

LITURGY IS THE WORK OF THE TRINITY

It would be difficult to overemphasize the notion that liturgy is the work of the people. As we have said, the liturgy is an action of the entire people of God as they exercise their share in the priesthood of Christ. Yet, while we rightly emphasize the human responsibility that liturgy entails, we cannot neglect the other side of the coin. Liturgy is the work of the people, but it is first—and foremost—the work of God.

This dual or reciprocal understanding of the liturgy as the work of God and the work of the people—as divine offering and human response—will be a constant element in our discussion of the Church's liturgy and her sacraments. In fact, one way we can describe liturgy and the sacraments is to say that they are special times when the divine and the human come together, when what is invisible takes on a form that allows it to be seen, experienced, understood, and responded to.

LITURGY IS THE WORK OF GOD THE FATHER

In the opening lines of the Letter to the Ephesians, the writer says that God is truly blessed, for "he chose us in Christ before the foundation of the world to be holy and

blameless before him" (1:4). The original Greek text of
this letter is even more significant, for it specifies what
God did for us through Christ: we are God's children
because God *adopted* us. As we shall see in our discussion
of infant Baptism, the concept of adoption is rich, indeed.
For now, we say that this act of adoption—an extraordinary act, undertaken solely at God's initiative—gave us as
pure gift a share in what Christ had by right and by
nature. We rejoice in all that we have because it was given
to us. That is why, even when we come together to celebrate the liturgy and the sacraments, and even though we
rightly emphasize that the liturgy is the work of the people, our celebration and prayer is first of all a response of
thanksgiving for the work God has done for us. It is no
accident that "Eucharist," the central liturgical action of
our Church, comes from the Greek word that means
"thanksgiving." To *be* thankful is the fundamental Christian *attitude*. To *give* thanks is the fundamental Christian
work.

The Father is the source of the liturgy, for the First
Person of the Trinity is the Father—the provider, the
giver—of all the blessings we enjoy:

> In the Church's liturgy the divine blessing is
> fully revealed and communicated. The Father is
> acknowledged and adored as the source and the
> end of all the blessings of creation and salvation.
> In his Word who became incarnate, died, and
> rose for us, he fills us with his blessings.
> Through his Word, he pours into our hearts the
> Gift that contains all gifts, the Holy Spirit.
> (*CCC*, #1082)

But just as the liturgy is the source and summit of all
the Church's activity, so is the Father not only the source
of the liturgy but also its goal. For the liturgy and the
sacraments are, first of all, our response to God's love and

work. A passage from the Preface for Weekdays IV in the *Sacramentary* expresses this well:

> You have no need of our praise, yet our desire
> to thank you is itself your gift. Our prayer of
> thanksgiving adds nothing to your greatness,
> but makes us grow in your grace, through Jesus
> Christ our Lord.

Through the liturgy we celebrate the blessings we have received from God. Through the liturgy, we offer God our gratitude, praise, and thanksgiving—and so continue to grow in God's grace. Again, this is the dual dimension, the reciprocal action, always present in our liturgical celebrations: our *recognition* of what we have been given, and our *response* to those gifts.

LITURGY IS THE WORK OF CHRIST THE SON

We mentioned above that through the liturgy and the sacraments, we participate in—and contribute to—the work of God. Indeed, we may consider Christ the "first sacrament" of God the Father. God so loved the world that he sent his Son: the clearest, most visible and, literally, most tangible sacrament (sign) of his love for the world. Christ is the sacrament that endures, for, in keeping with his promise in Matthew's Gospel, he does not abandon his disciples when he ascends into heaven, but fills them with the Holy Spirit so that "they [themselves] became sacramental signs of Christ" (*CCC* #1087).

This enduring presence of God's primary sacrament, Jesus Christ, suggests an essential difference between the "public works" of the Catholic Church and those, for example, of the Charitable Works Club across town. Both Church and club may perform many of the same public services, and they often may do so at the same time: leading a clothing drive for the poor during the Christmas season, for example, or providing meals or shelter for the homeless at Thanksgiving. Both services are public and both are needed services. The key difference, however, is—or should be—that the public service of the Church is done explicitly in the name of Jesus Christ. When it comes to the Church's charitable and apostolic works, we must answer two questions: "How can we meet people's needs?" and "How can we meet these people so that what we do for them we do clearly in the name of him in whom we are baptized?" To put it another way, Jesus assures us that we will always have the poor with us. When it comes to public works, the Church's task is to ensure that the poor know that Christ is always with them.

THE HOLY SPIRIT RECALLS AND MAKES PRESENT THE PERSON OF CHRIST

The Father is the source and goal of the Church's liturgy. Through the liturgy, we encounter God's great sacrament of love, Jesus Christ. *Anamnesis* and *epiclesis*, two technical words, suggest the action of the Holy Spirit in the Church's liturgy.

Anamnesis is remembering the past, a calling to mind the blessings God has bestowed upon humankind throughout the history of our salvation. Remembering is an essential part in liturgy and the sacraments. In every Eucharistic Prayer, for example, the preface and the subsequent narrative leading to the words of institution recall what it is God has done for us. One feature of the post-conciliar liturgy, in fact, is that in every sacramental celebration there is at least the opportunity to hear the Word of God—to hear, call to mind, and remember God's work for us in the past.

During the Eucharist, we also pray for God to "send [his] Spirit upon these gifts to make them holy." This is the *epiclesis*, the invocation of the Spirit to come down and instill power in the gifts of the Eucharist and in the lives of those celebrating. We come together as Church to "make" the Eucharist so that the Eucharist may make a difference in us as Church. Again, true liturgy is *work*:

> The Church therefore asks the Father to send the Holy Spirit to make the lives of the faithful a living sacrifice to God by their spiritual transformation into the image of Christ, by concern for the Church's unity, and by taking part in her mission through the witness and service of charity. (*CCC*, #1109)

LITURGY IS AN ENCOUNTER WITH GOD AND WITH THE CHURCH

The Catholic Church teaches that there are seven sacraments. And yet we might say that, ultimately, there are *two* great, fundamental sacraments. "God so loved the world that he gave his only Son" (John 3:16) is his primary sacrament, his greatest sign, of that love. And Christ, ever obedient to his Father's will, founded the Church to continue his presence and his saving work in and for the world. From these two great sacraments, Christ and the Church, come our seven sacraments: the most privileged and powerful of the Church's liturgical actions.

As we have said, to be baptized is to put aside forever the notion that our relationship with God is an exclusive, individual, private affair. The Church does the work of her liturgy and sacraments so that Christ's work and saving presence will continue to be made known to the world:

> The mission of the Holy Spirit in the liturgy of the Church is to prepare the assembly to encounter Christ; to recall and manifest Christ to the faith of the assembly; to make the saving work of Christ present and active by his

transforming power; and to make the gift of communion bear fruit in the Church. (*CCC*, #1112)

The liturgy and the sacraments are the great treasures of the Church. They are, however, treasures that often remain hidden. In the following chapter, we begin to consider how we might uncover, use, and share these riches we call sacraments—encounters with Christ in his Church.

CHAPTER SUMMARY

1. To be baptized is to put aside forever the notion that our relationship with God is strictly an exclusive, private matter. To be baptized is to be in communion, to be in the Church, and to do the work of the Church—liturgy.

2. The liturgy accomplishes "the work of our redemption" (*SC*, #2). It enables us to witness to others who we are because of what Christ has done for us. The liturgy does something *in* us, *for* us, *to* us, so that we may do something *in*, *for*, and *to* the world.

3. *Liturgy* comes from two Greek words that mean "the work of the people." Liturgy is an activity that supports the Church. Liturgy is the work "of the people": all are called to participate fully. And liturgy is *work*: it demands a response, not just observation.

4. As much as the liturgy and the sacraments are human responses, we must not forget that above all else liturgy is the work of Christ. We have liturgy for the same reason we have a Church: to carry on the work and continue to manifest the grace of Christ's death and resurrection. Liturgy and the sacraments are the premier place and time when heaven and earth come together. The Church does human things in the name

of Jesus Christ.

For Reflection

1. What, ideally, is the difference between a clothing drive for the poor that is sponsored by your parish and one that is sponsored by a neighborhood private club? How could this difference be expressed in practice? To take another example, how might the parish's service program for youth look different from the service program sponsored by the local school or civic community?

2. How can we more effectively promote the understanding that liturgy is the work of the entire people of God, and not the primary or exclusive domain of the clergy?

3. Another dictionary definition of *work* is that it is "something that has been done, made, or performed as a result of one's occupation, effort, or activity." Considering that the liturgy is "work," apply this as regards our liturgy.

4. Why should what we do in church make a difference in our lives when we leave church?

2 The Sacraments: the Church's "Visible Words"

KEY QUESTIONS

• What are sacraments?

• What are the essential parts of the sacramental rite?

• What do we mean when we say the sacraments are "visible words"?

• What does the Church ask of people—priest and parishioners—when they celebrate the sacraments?

AS WE BEGIN

• The word *sacrament* comes from the Latin *sacramentum*. As is often the case, this now religious word originally had a secular meaning. In early Rome the *sacramentum* was the pledge or oath that bound people engaging in financial transactions. The *sacramentum* also referred to a soldier's oath of loyalty to the emperor upon entering military service.

• The African theologian Tertullian (d. ca. 225) was the first writer to apply the word *sacramentum* to one of the Church's liturgical actions. He referred to Baptism as a *sacramentum*, understanding the pledge Christians took to be forever in the service of Christ as analogous to the loyalty owed the emperor by his soldiers.

14

One characteristic of our Roman Catholic Church is that we are a *sacramental* Church. Although God is invisible, we believe we can "see" God—we can sense the presence and the power of God—not only in our thoughts, but especially in and through the world and the people God has created.

In our Catholic tradition, the sacraments are among the privileged ways and means that God communicates himself to us. The sacraments are the primary ways we encounter Christ in his Church, are strengthened by God's grace, and are led by his Spirit. And, as we now begin to discuss, the sacraments are the main "verbs" of our Catholic Church and for our Christian lives.

WHAT ARE THE SACRAMENTS?

The traditional definition of a *sacrament*—"a visible sign instituted by Christ to give grace"—is familiar to all forty-something and older Catholics. This concise, nine-word definition contains three essential Church teachings concerning the sacraments: they are *signs*; they were *instituted*, or founded, *by Christ*; they *give grace*. This traditional definition speaks much truth but, like any simple statement, it cannot relate the whole truth.

As we begin our study of the sacraments, it may be helpful to offer a description of them, rather than a definition. Descriptions often help us understand something better than do definitions. Because descriptions use analogies and comparisons, they engage our imaginations as well as our analytical powers. Furthermore, descriptions encourage us to continue to explore what something is like, rather than be content merely with a correct, though somewhat abstract, statement of fact.

For example, when Joseph Martos titled his book on the history of the sacraments *Doors to the Sacred*, he provided us with a useful description of a sacrament. The sacraments have something to do with the *sacred* and, yes, they are doors to the sacred: avenues through which we can enter more fully into "God's house." Furthermore, the notion that the sacraments are doors suggests that while the sacraments offer us an opportunity to encounter the sacred, as is the case with real doors, we must walk through them to engage in this encounter. It is not enough to stand on the porch looking in.

Another helpful description of a sacrament comes from an artist musing on his craft. Asked to explain what purpose his image-laden writings served, the great American poet T.S. Eliot responded: "Poetry is not the assertion that something is true but the making of that truth more real to us" (as quoted in Bailey, Sally. "The Arts as an Avenue to the Spirit." *New Catholic World* **230** [1987]: p.264). Adapting Eliot's answer for our purposes, we offer a description of the sacraments: sacraments do not simply assert that something is true; they make that truth more real to us.

The sacraments are not merely statements of what we, as Catholics, believe. They are that, of course. But more importantly, the sacraments also try to make what we believe "more real" to us. When family and friends gather in the church vestibule on a Sunday afternoon to baptize one of their newborns, for example, they do not come together simply to talk about what they believe. They show what they believe by doing it: by taking part in a ritual that goes beyond the mere recital of words and into an engagement with gestures and actions, signs and symbols. When catechumens are sacramentally initiated into the Church at the solemn celebration of the Easter Vigil, they and their community are not only *professing* their belief that they are being reborn and are participating in Christ's death and resurrection. By acting out sacramentally what they believe, they are able, at a deeper level, to *experience* it as well. We believe God forgives us our sins. That belief is made more real to us, and more personal—in the case of Reconciliation—through our experience of celebrating the sacrament. And we do not simply tell the ill members of our family or parish that we care for them and will not abandon them in their suffering and illness. Rather, we put into action what we want to tell them by offering them visible words: we gather around them to pray for their health and well-being, impose hands upon them, and anoint them with holy oil.

THE SACRAMENTS ARE *OF* AND *FOR* THE CHURCH—NOT ONLY *IN* THE CHURCH

In the first chapter, I said that we must understand liturgy and the sacraments as *work*: as an activity requiring effort and perseverance. The sacraments are actions *of* the Church, actions the Church celebrates and effects in the name of Christ. The sacraments are also actions *for* the Church: they make the Church, bring her members together, and empower them to do what the Church does. The meaning and the power of the sacraments are not—and must not be—confined to those few moments we are "in" the church celebrating them.

To put it another way, the sacraments are not a kind of "sacred parenthesis" in the lives of Catholics. They are not the Christian's way of "calling time out," doing something holy, and then returning to "the real world." Rather, the sacraments are the "verbs" of our life; they are those actions, celebrated at special times and in special places, that show us how we are called to act all the time, in all places. We say that the sacraments are *of* and *for* the Church, because these sacred actions, ordinarily celebrated in the church building, are descriptions, orientations, guides—spiritual resources—for how we, the members of the Church, should live our lives. It is less important for us to define what a sacrament is than it is for us to understand how the sacraments should define us.

Our T.S. Eliot-adapted description of what sacraments are—not simply assertions of what we believe, but actions, visible words, that make what we believe "more real to us"—does not tell us everything about what the sacraments are and what they do. It does, however, convey the important concept that the sacraments are, in the words of the traditional definition, *visible signs*, signs that tell us— more importantly, signs that show us—what we believe.

In this chapter we examine in some detail what we mean by these visible words or "signs" that constitute a sacrament. The following two chapters explore, respectively, the Church teachings that the sacraments "give grace," and that they were "instituted," or founded, "by Christ."

THE SACRAMENTS ARE VISIBLE SIGNS

When we say the sacraments are visible signs, we are talking about that part of the sacrament we refer to as the ritual or the liturgical celebration: those things we say, hear, and do in church. Three things are involved in our consideration: the symbols or gestures used and the words spoken; the minister of the sacrament (ordinarily a priest, except in the case of Matrimony); and the recipients of the sacrament. Before we continue, however, a comment and a caution are in order, for here is a case where language can mislead.

It has long been the custom to speak of the sacraments' "ministers" (priests) and their "recipients" (parishioners). I continue to use those terms here, because they allow for an economy of words. What the terms do not suggest (and what I do not intend them to mean) is that those "receiving" the sacraments—adult catechumens who are baptized, for example, or adolescent boys and girls who are confirmed—are "passive participants." To "receive" a sacrament is not simply to be present, watching someone else (the priest) "do all the work." The sacraments are gifts but, unlike some gifts, to "receive" the gift of a sacrament is also to receive the responsibility that accompanies the gift. We discuss this further in the next chapter when we consider grace. For now, it is important to remember that we do not receive a sacrament and then walk away. Rather, we receive a sacrament so that we can walk in a different way.

Gestures, Symbols, and Words (Matter and Form)

When we celebrate the sacraments, we *do* things, we *use* things, and we *say* things. These things—whether done, used, or said—are referred to as the "matter" and "form" of the sacrament. The proper matter and form are one of three things required for the valid celebration of a sacrament—that is, for the Church to recognize and acknowledge these particular actions as "one of her own."

When applied to the sacraments, the concepts of matter and form come from the Scholastic theologians (eleventh through the fourteenth centuries). These scholars were trying to define exactly what it was that made up a sacrament. They found a helpful tool in Aristotle's understanding of how the world is put together. For him, matter and form were the basic building blocks of the universe. *Matter* refers to the raw material that can be used to make something—a lump of clay, for example, or a pile of lumber. *Form* refers to the particular way the raw material is used: the clay is "formed" into a bowl, or the lumber is measured, cut, and put together to "form" a desk or a table.

Table One in Appendix I displays the matter and form— the basic building blocks of the liturgical actions—of the seven sacraments. In reference to the table (and to the concept of matter and form) there are several things to note. First, the matter—usually a gesture or a symbol—can, by itself, be ambiguous. An anointing with oil constitutes the matter of two sacraments, for example, and in fact an anointing is also part of the celebration of the sacraments of Baptism and Holy Orders. That is why the words of the sacrament—the sacramental *form*ula—are most important. As explanatory words, they define more clearly what the particular actions or symbols mean. And as words of faith, they are words of prayer, and so they call upon God to carry out or effect what it is that the actions and symbols express or signify.

A second thing to remember when reviewing Table One is that, while we consider the proper matter and form to be among those elements necessary for a sacrament to be considered valid, this does not mean that matter and form constitute a sacramental celebration. When we baptize infants, for example, we not only pour water over their foreheads (matter) and say the formula (form), but we also anoint them with oil, clothe them in a white garment, present their parents with a candle, read from the Scriptures, and say a number of prayers for them and their parents. All of these gestures and words are part of the sacrament; they tell us—they show us—what it is we believe is taking place at this Baptism. In the same way, while the proper words (form) must be said over bread and wine (matter) for the valid celebration of the Eucharist, the Eucharist is more than having the proper matter and reciting the correct form. The sacrament of the Eucharist calls a community together to pray and to listen to, reflect upon, and respond to the Word of God. We say that matter and form are most essential, not because they are all there is to a sacrament, but because they are the key elements—the primary gestures, symbols, and words—that define most clearly what it is we believe Christ is effecting and we are celebrating in this particular liturgical action. Without them the central truth of what we believe (and the central action of Christ that the Church is sacramentally effecting) would not be visible—and so the sacrament, the visible words, would not be present.

Finally, note that in two sacraments—Reconciliation and Matrimony—the proper matter is neither a symbol nor a gesture, properly speaking, but the attitude or disposition of those engaging in (and not just "receiving") the sacrament.

The symbols and gestures of our sacramental celebrations are not in themselves mysterious, and they certainly are not magical. Oil, water, bread and wine, touch: these are among the most basic of human realities. As human beings, we are creatures who communicate largely through symbols. The symbols we use most often are words, but these are not the only ones. Our bodies themselves are symbols of who we are, ways through which people encounter our spirit, our soul, our heart (see *CCC*, #1084).

We give further consideration to the communicative power of symbols in the next chapter when we discuss "how" the sacraments confer grace. For now, it is enough to understand that the matter and form express the core meaning of the sacrament.

In addition to being the primary "expressive tools" of a sacramental rite, matter and form suggest an important theological teaching about the sacraments. The sacraments, instituted by Christ, are among the ways the Church, Christ's Body on Earth, continues the Incarnation—continues to make the love and grace God offered us through Christ more present, more real, to us. Through the sacraments the divine (Christ's presence) takes on a form we can see and touch (bread and wine). Another way of describing the sacraments then, is to say that the sacraments bring together the earthly and the divine. We begin with matter, the things of this world. But when the word of faith is added, a "door to the sacred" is opened.

Of course, sacraments involve more than "signs," no matter how expressive or sacred they are. *Sacramenta propter homines*, as one theological idiom puts it: "the sacraments are for people." This means much more than the fact that we do not administer the sacraments to the dead. It means that the sacraments are for our benefit; God does not need the sacraments to act on our behalf. While we are on this earth, however, we need these visible words, these "doors to the sacred," that help us discover the "hidden treasures" of God's grace and love. Our celebration of the sacraments does not allow God to do something that otherwise God would not be able to do. Rather, the celebration helps us to understand and experience what it is God offers us.

We have been discussing the importance of the matter and form of the sacraments, and have said that the proper use of them is among the requirements for the valid celebration of a sacrament. There are two other requirements and, given our insistence that the liturgy is the work of the people, it should come as no surprise that these further requirements concern people: the "minister" of the sacraments and those who "receive" the sacraments. (Recall our previously expressed dissatisfaction with the technical terms "minister" and "recipient.")

The Minister

What does the Church require of her ministers (ordinarily priests) when they preside over a sacramental celebration? The answer, blunt as it may seem, is not much. Primarily, the minister must intend to do "what the Church does." That is, he must intend to administer the Church's sacrament of Baptism, Reconciliation, Eucharist, etc. For a sacrament to be validly celebrated—that is, for a sacrament to be celebrated in such a way that the Church would recognize this action as "one of her own"—it is not necessary that the minister understand everything there is to know about the theology of the sacrament. Nor does the minister necessarily have to believe in every aspect of the Church's teaching regarding the sacrament. Finally, the minister does not have to be in the "state of grace" himself to validly preside over the celebration of a sacrament. A priest, conscious of being in the state of mortal sin, can still hear the confessions of his parishioners and absolve them of their sins—even sins of which he himself might be guilty.

Considering the sacraments in this way may seem as though we are reducing them to objects, to magic moments, to play-acting, or to the bare minimum. On the contrary, these requirements of the minister (and they are minimal requirements) have a long history, dating back to the fifth century when Saint Augustine (d. 430) was engaged in a bitter debate with a group called the Donatists. Briefly, the Donatists believed that a minister of the sacraments could not give others what he himself did not have. For example, if a priest defected from the faith during a time of persecution, he forfeited his own Baptism; thus, the people he baptized after his defection had not really been baptized. According to the Donatists, the priest had left the Church: obviously his Baptism had not been effective; it did not really "take." Since that priest no longer had the grace of Baptism, he could not pass that baptismal grace on to someone else. Furthermore, so the argument went, if the priest had a change of heart and wanted to rejoin the Church, he would have to be re-baptized—as would all those he had baptized.

Augustine's response to the Donatists provided several key teachings about the sacraments. The one most relevant to our discussion here is that the grace of the sacrament comes through Christ, not through the priest. Negatively put, the unworthiness (or even the unorthodoxy)

of the minister does not hinder the sacrament from conferring the grace it "contains." *Christus auctor sacramento-*
rum, as Saint Ambrose (d. 397) said: it is not the human
minister but Christ who is the "authority, the power,"
behind the sacraments. In this sense, we can say that just
as Christ is the fundamental sacrament of God's love for
the world, so is Christ also the fundamental minister of
every sacramental celebration that continues to make
known the power of his presence among us. This is what
the Church means when she teaches that the sacraments
confer grace *ex opere operato* ("through the work
worked")—a point we discuss in the next chapter.

The Donatist controversy is not entirely dead; it creeps
up in many parishes today in subtle ways. I remember a
conversation some years ago with my father, a permanent
deacon, and one of our Catholic neighbors. The neighbor
said that he would not receive Communion at the hands of
anyone but a priest, because only with a priest was he sure
he was dealing with a man of grace. Besides not improving
his relationship with my father, our neighbor was mistaken
on several counts. First, being ordained a priest is to
receive a state of objective holiness from the Church, but
it does not guarantee that the priest is always in the state
of grace. Second, whether or not the priest is in the state
of grace has no effect on the real presence of Christ
received in the Eucharist—or, as should be clear from the
above discussion, on the valid transubstantiation of the
bread and wine into the Body and Blood of Christ. Finally,
it is always the grace and power of Christ, and not that of
the minister, that is offered through the celebration of the
sacraments. Christ is the fundamental sacrament. Christ is
the primary minister of, the authority behind, the sacraments. The sacraments are encounters with Christ
through the Church.

The Recipient

Just as there are minimum requirements for the minister, there are minimum requirements for the persons receiving the sacraments. Adults approaching Baptism, for example, need not understand everything there is to know about the history and theology of Baptism in the Catholic Church. They do need to approach the sacrament of their own free will, however, and they need to have at least a minimal, basic understanding of what Baptism does: that it frees them from their sins, gives them a new life in Christ, and brings them into the Catholic Church. Persons approaching the confessional do not need to know everything (or anything) about the penitential controversies in the early Church, or about the doctrines of justification and redemption. However, they do have to approach the sacrament freely and contritely. They must intend to confess at least all the mortal sins of which they are conscious, and they must have the intention of trying to do their best to avoid those sins in the future.

There are two exceptions, or special cases, concerning the disposition of the recipient. The first, and most frequent, concerns the Baptism of infants. Other than perhaps howling, an infant brings no disposition to the font. Rather, the parents bring their infant freely and in fact, as we will discuss in a subsequent chapter, it is *their* faith that in large part justifies the Baptism of their infant. A second exception concerns the Anointing of the Sick when it is celebrated for the benefit of an unconscious person.

Although contemporary theology treats this sacrament as an anointing *of the sick* rather than the last anointing (Extreme Unction) of someone dying, there are times when anointing an unconscious person is appropriate. The understanding is that if it is reasonable to presume that the person would have wanted to celebrate the sacrament, the sacrament may be celebrated. The Scholastic theologians, to whom we are indebted for much of this scientific analysis of the sacraments, would agree that neither the infant nor the unconscious person has what we would understand as an "open disposition." The point, however, was that the howling infant and the comatose adult had placed no barrier or obstacle to their receiving the sacrament.

While these two cases may seem somewhat exceptional, they demonstrate an important rule, or truth, about the sacraments. Human weakness, even human inability to understand that God is acting on our behalf or to respond to that action, does not prevent God from offering us grace and love.

The Bare Minimum Is Not the Ideal

In discussing the three elements required for a celebration to be considered a valid sacrament, we are not talking about the ideal way the sacrament should be celebrated. The ideal celebration of the Eucharist does not take place by simply putting bread and wine on the altar and having a bored and sleepy priest pronounce the words of institution while parishioners freely, but disinterestedly, look on. Proper matter and form, the intention of the minister, and the disposition of the recipient are the minimal requirements that must be met for the Church to recognize this particular action as one of her sacraments.

Historically, the emphasis on the importance of these requirements came from the Scholastic theologians. As theology became more of a science, its "doctors" analyzed the sacramental acts and their effects with greater precision. Today, some of their concerns may appear a bit pedantic—their interest, for example, in exactly when the bread and wine become the Body and Blood of Christ, or the precise effects of the Anointing of the Sick. For the most part, their interest lay in trying to determine the importance of the sacramental signs, symbols, gestures, and words, and what effect these celebrations actually had in the lives of people.

The concern for sacramental validity has implications most often when one or both spouses seek to have their marriage annulled. Canonically, an annulment is the Church's judgment declaring that the sacrament of Matrimony between this man and this woman never existed, i.e., that what was required for a valid sacrament was not present. Table One in Appendix I shows clearly on what grounds most marriages are annulled: the proper matter and form—in the case of Matrimony, the mutual exchange of vows, given with full consent and freedom—were absent. And if this is the case, then obviously we can question the intention of the ministers (the bride and the groom are the ministers of the sacrament of Matrimony) as well as the disposition of the recipients. (For additional examples, consult the entry "validity" in the Glossary.)

THE POWER OF SACRAMENTAL WORDS AND SYMBOLS

The concern over proper gestures, symbols, and words reminds us that these elements of our sacramental celebrations are important. While the Scholastic theologians may have had scientific, theological precision in mind, we should take care that the symbols and gestures we use clearly express what they point to. Long, detailed explanations of sacramental signs belong in a classroom or in pre- or postsacramental instruction, not as a running commentary during the rite itself. After all, if a symbol has to be explained at great length so that people will understand what it symbolizes, then something has gone awry.

The words of the sacramental rite, especially those words that are considered the form of the sacrament, are most important. It is these "spoken words" that give form and meaning to the "visible words" of the symbols and gestures. It is for this reason that the Church provides the essential words, rather than relying upon the education, imagination, or ability of the priest. That is why, as the *CCC* states, "no sacramental rite may be modified or manipulated at the will of the minister or the community" (#1125). The sacraments do not "belong" to a particular minister or a particular community; they belong to the Church because they are actions of the Church.

We have been discussing the three requirements that must be present for the valid celebration of a sacrament. The Church teaches that through the valid celebration of a sacrament, grace is conferred *ex opere operato* ("through the work worked") or by virtue of the celebration of the sacrament.

But what, exactly, is *ex opere operato*? What do we mean by "grace"? And how do we move beyond a "bare minimum" understanding of our involvement in the celebration of the sacraments? These are among the questions we consider in the next chapter.

CHAPTER SUMMARY

1. The sacraments are "doors to the sacred," "visible words" that lead us to hidden treasures. The sacraments do not merely tell us that something is true; they also try to make more real to us that which we believe.

2. The sacraments are not "holy moments" of our lives. Rather, they are the instruments through which our lives may become holy. The sacraments are the "verbs" of Christian life, not its "parenthetical comments." We do not receive a sacrament and then walk away. Rather, we celebrate the sacraments so that we can walk in a different way.

3. Ordinarily the matter of a sacrament is the symbol or gesture that expresses what lies at the core of the sacramental celebration. The form, or the essential words of prayer and faith, further defines and specifies what the symbol or gesture expresses.

4. A sacrament is considered valid if three requirements are met: the use of the proper matter and form, the minister intending to do what the Church intends in celebrating this sacrament, and recipients approaching the sacrament of their own free will.

5. Christ is the fundamental sacrament. Christ is the primary minister of, the authority behind, the sacraments. The sacraments belong to the Church, and not to any one minister or community.

FOR REFLECTION

1. You are helping parents prepare for their children's first celebration of Reconciliation or Eucharist, and you want to emphasize that a sacrament is an action that makes what we believe more real to us. What examples of symbols or family traditions from the parents' own experience could you draw upon to do this?

2. Reviewing Table One in Appendix I and considering the matter and form of each of the seven sacraments, what is the core meaning of the sacramental action expressed by these symbols, gestures, and words?

3. What does it mean to say, "Christ is the fundamental sacrament?" What does it mean to say that, when we celebrate a sacrament, Christ is the fundamental minister?

3 The Sacraments and Grace: Discovering Hidden Treasures

KEY QUESTIONS

• What is grace?

• How do we "receive" grace from the sacraments?

• What happens to the grace we receive?

• Are the sacraments *instruments* or *symbols* of grace?

AS WE BEGIN

• A traditional, systematic study of grace would offer various classifications and subgroupings of the different "kinds" of grace. The Church teaches that there are two primary kinds of grace: sanctifying grace (given first at Baptism) and actual grace (given when we need it). Sacramental grace, conferred through the celebration of the sacraments, is a derivative of sanctifying grace. We will forgo an analysis of grace in favor of a more descriptive approach.

• The *Catechism of the Catholic Church* offers brief but excellent treatments of grace and related concepts: justification (#1987–1995), grace (#1996–2005), merit (#2006–2011), and Christian holiness (#2012–2016).

The sacraments are "visible signs instituted by Christ *to give grace*." But what is this "grace" that the sacraments give?

Many times we tend to think of grace as a "thing" that fills our souls. I remember an illustration from my childhood catechism that depicted my soul as a bottle, sacraments as a milk carton, and grace as the nourishing white liquid flowing from carton to bottle. (Correspondingly, sin was shown as dirt that turned the white milk into an ugly brown, leaving stains on the bottle.)

Contemporary Catholic reflection tries to avoid understanding grace as a *thing*. In fact, to talk about grace is to talk about God. The more we understand grace, the more we understand what a *grac*ious God we have. Considering grace as a thing, as an object, does not do justice to the great gift of and from God that grace is.

WHAT IS GRACE?

Grace is God's favor; grace is participation in God's life. Let us give further consideration to each of these statements.

GRACE IS GOD'S FAVOR, GOD'S FREE AND UNDESERVED HELP

Again, a definition from a secular dictionary is a good place to start. *Grace* is "favor," and *favor* is "a gracious, kind, or friendly attitude" or "an act evidencing such an attitude." Thus grace is not a thing that comes from God, but is an act of God that shows us something of who God is. To "receive grace" is to experience God acting—for our good—in our lives.

Essential to the concept of grace is the understanding that grace is a gift from God. Unfortunately, too many times we think of grace more as a paycheck, as something

God gives us because we have met our part of the bargain by doing something good. But grace is not something we earn. Grace is neither a bribe to entice us to do good, nor a reward for the good we do. Grace is not something we deserve, but is something we need. And because of our need, grace is offered to us out of God's love, not because of our merit.

GRACE IS PARTICIPATION IN THE LIFE OF GOD

Grace is our share in the very life of God! Grace is one way God offers his life to us and, in so doing, offers us our identity: we are God's adopted children. (The theological concept of "adoption" is an exceptionally rich one for understanding our relationship with God and for appreciating how that relationship came about. We refer to our "adoption by God" several times in Chapter 5, in our discussion of Baptism. Appendix II offers a reflection on our status as "God's adopted sons and daughters.")

We often speak of a particular moment as a "time of grace," or we look upon a special incident as a "moment of grace." What we mean in both instances is that at these times or moments we were, in some way, for some reason, more aware than usual of God's presence in our lives. (Recall our fundamental description of sacraments: that they are not just statements of fact, but visible words that try to make what we believe more real to us.) In addition to offering us God's grace, the sacraments try to help us experience that grace more concretely, more realistically, in our lives. The more we experience the power of God's grace working in our lives, the more we will do good—not so that we *will receive grace*, but because we *enjoy* God's grace.

WHAT ALLOWS US TO RESPOND TO GRACE? *GRACE!*

Grace is a gift from God, given freely at God's initiative, unmerited and undeserved by us. But this free gift does not come cheap. Grace is, in one sense, a gift given with strings attached. The strings are the connections we have with God, the relationship with God made possible by grace, and so our *response* to God's grace.

What allows us to respond to God's grace? The answer is: God's grace. God's grace acts in us even before we realize it—one reason why we find it sacramentally sensible and credible to baptize infants, even though the children are unaware of what we are "doing to them." As the history of our salvation shows, God does not wait until we are ready, until we are prepared (and certainly not until we are deserving), to offer us grace. Rather, God gives us grace so that we may know—and respond further—to the grace we are given.

Psalm 139, which inspired Francis Thompson's magnificent poem titled "The Hound of Heaven," is a wonderful depiction of this. In the poem, God is not one who remains in his heavens, waiting for his creatures to some day come to their senses and acknowledge him as their Creator and giver of life. Despite what we may sometimes think or feel, our God never "takes a day off" from our lives. God is the relentless pursuer, forever after us, always trying to catch our attention. The psalm paints a similar picture of an all-present, ever-pursuing God (and with images that remind us that the Psalms are, indeed, the Bible's "poetry"):

> You hem me in, behind and before,
>   And lay your hand upon me.
>
> Where can I go from your spirit?
>   Or where can I flee from your presence?
> If I ascend to heaven, you are there;
>   if I make my bed in Shē'ōl, you are there.
> If I take the wings of the morning

and settle at the farthest limits of the sea,
Even there your hand shall lead me,
    And your right hand shall hold me fast.
(Psalm 139:5, 7–10; NRSV translation)

We may also consider grace as the *effect* of God's acting
on our behalf. In other words, because of this particular
moment or time "of grace," we were able to do something
different, be someone better, than we ordinarily are or
would be capable of if left to our abilities alone. Reflecting
upon grace then, we might ask: "How am I different (pre-
sumably, how am I better) because of what God has done
for me?"

Finally, we might consider grace as a measure of the
depth of our relationship with God. In this way of thinking, our concern is not for the state of grace we may or
may not be in, but how we can continue to deepen that
state, that relationship. "How close am I to God? How can
I deepen my love for God?" are questions we might ask.

THE SACRAMENTS CONFER GRACE

In the sixteenth century, the Council of Trent defined certain teachings of the Church. While that Council affirmed
that the sacraments did give grace, it refrained from specify-
ing exactly how or in what manner grace was given. That
was a legitimate question, the Council believed, one that
merited continuing discussion among Catholic theologians.

How do the sacraments confer grace? A number of theological theories have been offered. The most popular for
many centuries, as well as the one perhaps most familiar to
Catholics, is the theory of *physical* or *instrumental causality*,
proposed by Thomas Aquinas. According to this theory,
the sacraments are the reservoirs of and the pipelines for
grace in much the same way that a lake holds water and its
rivers bring the water inland (or, referring to our previous

example, as the carton pours the milk into the bottle). God "places" grace in the sacraments, and the sacraments make that grace available to us.

Moral causality is another theory, taught by John Duns Scotus (d. 1308), a Franciscan theologian of the Scholastic period. He suggested that when people celebrate a sacrament, the sacramental celebration reminds God of his love for humankind; God then gives his grace directly to those asking for it. Centuries later, a modern Scholastic, L. Billot (d. 1931), proposed yet another theory. Unlike Scotus's teaching of moral causality, in which the sacrament had an effect upon God, Billot's theory of *intentional causality* suggested that the sacraments had an effect first upon those celebrating them. By celebrating the sacraments, people became disposed—their hearts were opened—to receive grace.

These and other theories are not "wrong." Each tells us something important about the sacraments, God, and ourselves. For example, Aquinas's teaching reminds us that the sacraments do confer grace—or that they contain and can open up for us the hidden treasures of God's grace. Scotus's reasoning, that the sacraments have an effect upon God, reminds us that our sacramental celebrations are occasions of praising and thanking God. And Billot is certainly correct when he says that our experience of celebrating the sacraments can help us experience further the grace God offers us. Each of these theories can help us understand how to grow in God's grace and love. Like many theological reflections, each theory suggests part of the truth, but not necessarily the whole truth—something difficult to do, after all, when we are considering the mystery of God. (For example, the Council of Trent condemned a teaching, similar to Billot's, proposed by some of the Protestant Reformers, that the sacraments only nourished faith; they did not confer grace.)

THE SACRAMENTS AS SYMBOLIC CAUSES OF GRACE

How do the sacraments confer grace? Another theory, perhaps the most prevalent today, is that, as symbolic actions, the sacraments confer grace *in the manner according to symbols*. That is, the sacraments communicate to us more concretely that which we cannot see, that which we would be less aware of, that which we could not experience, without the benefit of the symbolic action. Again, the sacraments don't simply tell us what we believe; rather, they try to make what we believe more real to us.

The question is often asked: "Well, are the sacraments instruments of grace, or are they merely symbols of grace?" This question often assumes that the answer is one *or* the other. Furthermore, if the response is "the sacraments symbolize grace," then the charge is sometimes made that we are reducing the sacraments to "mere symbols." Some comments are in order.

First, the more we understand the actual power of a symbol, the less we will be inclined to place the word "merely" in front of it. Symbols are not signs that give us facts or pieces of information—after which we go on our way and dismiss them from our minds. For example, no one spends more time than is necessary looking at a clock or a traffic light or a class schedule, yet these things are signs. They give us the information we need, but they do nothing *to* us (unless the clock is actually a third-generation heirloom, in which case it has become more a symbol of significant meaning than a simple transmitter of information).

Symbols make the truth more real to us through the actions that accompany them. Symbols engage our imaginations and our souls, not only our minds (the way a clock or traffic light does). A symbol begins with what we believe and places it in front of us. Or, better, because of the way a symbol can engage us, it makes us more present to the reality that is already (and always) there.

We don't approach a symbol to get information, as we do signs. Rather, we encounter a symbol so that we will be conformed to—formed more into—the reality the symbol is and communicates.

A Lesson about the Power of Symbols

I had just begun studying sacramental theology at the graduate level when I encountered the absolute and magnificent power of symbols—and this lesson was not one I learned in a classroom. I had been in Rome for some five months: long enough to have become acclimated to my new environs, certainly long enough to feel homesick. There were many things I loved about Rome: the food, the history, the monuments, the churches—just the experience of being in Rome. But I am American through and through, and so one drizzly February day, as I was walking down narrow, garbage-cluttered side streets, all I could think about was how much I wanted a real taste of America—in the form of a couple of hamburgers and French fries.

I really didn't know exactly where in the city I was during that walk. I was just wandering, passing time, trying to fight off "American-itis." As I rounded a corner and came out onto a major boulevard, I looked up—and stopped dead in my tracks. There, a few hundred feet in front of me, was the American embassy. And there, on the grounds, fluttered the American flag—the first American flag I had seen in almost half a year.

I've never considered myself a rabid patriot, but the vision of that flag—the symbol of my country, my friends, and so much of my life—had a profound effect upon me at that moment. For a while I was home. Or, more precisely, home was present to me once again. Home was made *more real* to me. At that moment, and for some time afterwards, the American flag was not simply a three-colored piece of cloth.

Symbols explain how things or persons are and can be present, not how they are absent—or not present in the way we would prefer them to be.

SACRAMENTS: SYMBOLS *OR* CAUSES OF GRACE?

The question remains: do the sacraments confer grace—or are they "merely" symbols of that grace? Given the power of symbols, the answer is: *the sacraments do both*. They confer grace *and* they symbolize the conferring of that grace. This is what the Scholastic formula meant when it said that the sacraments effect (cause) what they signify, and that they signify what they effect.

Another example of how symbols "work" may help clarify this, and help us better understand how a sacrament can both "effect what it signifies and signify what it effects." The example, admittedly a graphic one, is marital sexual intercourse. (I trust it will not be judged disrespectful to use marital intercourse as an analogy, an illustration, of how sacraments both symbolize and effect God's grace. Recall that Matrimony is not only a sacrament but also an image specifically used to symbolize—to make more real—the relationship between God and his people or between Christ and his Church, as the prophet Hosea and the Letter to the Ephesians, respectively, suggest.)

One of the most beautiful, intense moments a loving and faithful husband and wife share is their coming together to be one flesh. But how would we categorize these moments? Is sexual intercourse an act—or is it a symbol? The answer is: the act of sexual intercourse is *both*.

Intercourse between husband and wife expresses—signifies—the love they already share, and so is a *symbol* of the relationship that does in fact exist. But their sexual intercourse not only reflects the love between them, it also continues to contribute to—effect—the love they profess for each other. This act and symbol of sexual intercourse, of course, does not express all there is about their marriage, nor is it the only cause or expression of their love. But it is a particularly intense action that both symbolizes and effects their entire relationship.

I offer one final observation proceeding from this powerful example of how an action can be both symbol and cause. Sexual intercourse between husband and wife is also a response—a response to the love between man and woman that brought them together, that joins them now, and that will guide them into their future, together. We refer to the *CCC* and its comment about the past, present, and future history made real through the celebration of the sacraments, about the love that exists even before we are aware of it, and about our subsequent response to that love.

> Since Pentecost, it is through the sacramental signs of his Church that the Holy Spirit carries on the work of sanctification. The sacraments of the Church do not abolish but purify and integrate all the richness of the signs and symbols of the cosmos and of social life. Further, they fulfill the types and figures of the Old Covenant, signify and make actively present the salvation wrought by Christ, and prefigure and anticipate the glory of heaven. (#1152)

THE SACRAMENTS CONFER *EX OPERE OPERATO. EX OPERE OPERATO?*

The Latin phrase *ex opere operato* means, literally, "by the work worked." *Ex opere operato* (or *opus operatum*) is a technical theological expression that tells us, concisely, that "if the right rites are rightly done," then grace is conferred through the very celebration of the sacrament.

This concept can be—indeed, often has been—poorly understood. It is poorly understood if it encourages the attitude that "all I need do is go to confession and my sins are forgiven and that's that." Understanding *ex opere opera-to* in this way suggests that the sacraments are magic, the priest has to say only a few words and it's all taken care of. The parishioner can say, "I really don't even have to pay attention" or the priest can say, "It doesn't matter if I say these prayers reverently or not, God will take care of it." Attitudes such as this foster an impersonal, mechanical approach to the sacraments. The rituals become akin to vending machines: we drop in a few coins, pull back the knob, and get what we paid for. Simple to do, not much to think about. As the saying goes, "Whatever happened to the good old days when you could go to church and not have a blessed thought?" Fortunately, nothing could be further from actual Church teaching.

Ex opere operato, properly understood, is the "guarantee" that when we approach the sacraments in faith (the correct disposition) and if the minister celebrates the ritual prop-erly, God's grace is conferred and our relationship with Christ and with the Church is affirmed or established:

> From the moment that a sacrament is celebrat-ed in accordance with the intention of the Church, the power of Christ and his Spirit acts in and through it, independently of the personal holiness of the minister. Nevertheless, the fruits of the sacraments also depend on the disposition of the one who receives them. (#1128)

We will return to that last sentence in a moment, for it is essential to our proper understanding of what *ex opere operato* means—and what it does not mean. Concerning the rest of the citation, we are again in that conversation among my father, our neighbor, and me that I recounted in the previous chapter. Or perhaps we are reviewing the question recently appearing on the question-and-answer section of a Catholic web page. The questioner was concerned because she had learned that the priest who confirmed her husband and baptized their infant was, at that very time, thinking of leaving the priesthood and, in fact, was living in a state of sin. This priest was not in the state of grace, the woman observed, and so did that mean that the important sacraments her family had received "did not take"? In response, Church teaching makes it unambiguously clear: the power or effectiveness of a sacrament—that is, of what God has done through Christ and what Christ continues to do through his Church—does not depend upon the holiness (or the lack thereof) of the minister. The sacraments receive their power through Christ. The sacraments are powerful actions because they are founded in the person and life of Christ.

AND THEN THERE IS *EX OPERE OPERANTIS*

To say that the sacraments are effective *ex opere operato*, however, is only the starting point of sacramental theology. As mentioned, grace—God's gift—is given freely. But looking at it from another perspective, we can say that for the sacraments to work, Catholics must work at the sacraments. This introduces another technical distinction in sacramental theology: the distinction between a sacrament's *effectiveness* on one hand, and the sacrament's *fruitfulness* on the other.

To say, as I did above, that "for the sacraments to work, Catholics must work at the sacraments" is not to negate the teaching that the sacraments are effective *ex opere operato:* that it is Christ as the primary minister of the sacrament, Christ as the primary power behind the sacraments, who guarantees the conferral of grace. But to recall another previous comment, the sacraments are not meant to be "parenthetical comments" in our lives. The sacraments are "verbs," words of action, words of commitment. This is what the concluding sentence of the *CCC*'s paragraph cited above means (#1128).

Ex opere operantis (or *opus operantis*) is the Church teaching that both complements and completes the teaching of *ex opere operato*. This new phrase means "by the work of the worker," and it refers to the person receiving the sacraments. The sacraments are effective—they confer grace—"by the work worked" (*ex opere operato*). But the sacraments are fruitful in a person's life—they really are the "verbs" of the Christian's life—only to the extent that we take advantage of them and put them to use. To refer to our previous images and descriptions of sacraments, if a door to the sacred is opened, we still need to walk through it; if we discover the hidden treasure, we must open it; if the truth has become more real to us, we are in a better position to respond to it. To put it as concisely as possible: the sacraments offer us grace as a gift. Our response—our *responsibility*—is to unwrap that gift and put it to good use. *Ex opere operato*—the sacrament's effectiveness—guarantees that a sacrament is an encounter with Christ and his grace through our Church. *Ex opere operantis*—the sacrament's fruitfulness—depends upon the extent to which we unwrap the gift and use it.

A SACRAMENT IS AN ENCOUNTER WITH CHRIST—AND WITH CHRIST'S CHURCH

A liturgical celebration confers grace—what we may call the spiritual, or religious, effect of the sacrament. Grace is the ultimate effect of the sacraments, because our ultimate destiny is to be in union with God.

But the sacraments are actions of Christ *through the Church*. And, as we have observed, if we may consider Christ as the primary or fundamental sacrament of God, then the Church is the primary or fundamental sacrament of Christ. In line with this, sacraments confer grace, the religious effect, and they establish us in a certain relationship with the visible Church—what we will call the "ecclesial effect."

We referred briefly to this in the preceding chapter when we discussed some of the important contributions Saint Augustine offered to Catholic sacramental theology. Among these—again, the context is his theological battle with the Donatists—is that, while sacraments confer grace, which can certainly be lost or forfeited, some of the sacraments also confer something that cannot be lost. This ecclesial effect is also called the *sacramental character*. Traditionally this has been understood as the indelible, invisible seal placed upon the soul by the sacraments of Baptism, Confirmation, and Holy Orders. While the grace (religious effect) of these sacraments can be lost (the gift can remain unwrapped), the character (ecclesial effect) remains always. From a pastoral perspective, this is why these three sacraments can never be repeated once they are validly received.

The sacramental character is both a "reality" in itself and a "symbol," or sign, of another reality. For example, Baptism is incorporation into both Christ and the Church. Membership in the Church is a reality; it is also a sign of our incorporation into Christ. As it has come to be understood and frequently practiced today, Confirmation "seals" or completes Christian initiation. The person confirmed receives from the Church "the power to profess faith in Christ publicly and as it were officially" (St. Thomas Aquinas, *Summa Theologica* III, 72, 5 *ad* 2)—a reality in itself—which is also a sign or symbol.

Similarly, Holy Orders confers upon the priest visible status, authority, and power (all for the sake of service) within the Church—a reality in itself—which is also a sign, or symbol, of another of the sacrament's effects, namely, that the priest is configured to Christ and so can act in his name—in the person of Christ as Head of his Body, the Church.

The Scholastic theologians spoke of the other four sacraments—Reconciliation, Eucharist, Anointing, and Matrimony—as conferring grace and a certain "adornment of the soul." This is less important to us here, but applying the concept to the sacrament of Reconciliation offers us another way of understanding "character" as denoting both reality and symbol, as reminding us that a sacrament both symbolizes something and effects, or causes, something. In the case of sacramental Reconciliation, for example, the "ecclesial" effect of the sacrament is that one is reconciled with the Church. This is a reality in itself—and is also a symbol of another reality: the "religious" effect of the sacrament, that one is reconciled with God.

The sacraments are among the greatest gifts in our Catholic tradition. But, as the *Catechism* says, the Church only "gradually recognized this treasure received from Christ" (#1117). Indeed, each of the seven sacraments has a history that is as complex as it is interesting. We will consider some of the more important aspects of this history in the following chapter.

CHAPTER SUMMARY

I have introduced a good deal of technical theological vocabulary and concepts in this chapter. Rather than offering a list of conclusions, perhaps it would be refreshing and practical to summarize our discussion by considering two Gospel parables. Our reflection on these parables may, like the celebration of the sacraments, make the truth more real to us.

After spending a few moments reading and reflecting on each parable, readers are invited to assess—and add to—the reflections I offer here, in the context of our discussion in this chapter. This "assignment" may be considered an addition to the "For Reflection" points that conclude this chapter.

THE PARABLE OF THE PRODIGAL SON (LUKE 15:11–32)

When the younger son "came to himself" (v. 17), he began to prepare the speech of repentance he will give to his father, hoping that his father will allow him back into the house. The son plans to say three things: that he has sinned against heaven and against his father; that he is no longer worthy to be called his father's son; and that he hopes the father will allow him back into the house at least as a hired hand.

But the son never gets a chance to finish his speech! As soon as he concludes the second part—"I am no longer worthy to be called your son" (v. 21)—his father interrupts him, and will not allow the son to continue to deny the relationship that is theirs (father and son, not father and slave). This surely is grace: an act of benevolence that is unearned, unmerited, and certainly not given as a reward for good behavior. It is also a reflection of what we mean by "sacramental character," that indelible, lasting mark that establishes us in a visible and permanent relationship with the Church and with God. By squandering his father's inheritance (can we call this "baptismal grace"?), the younger son certainly abused and so lost the gift his father had given him. But he never lost the identity given him by his father. He remained his father's son, even though he did not always act as a son should. The father does not "make him a son again." He brings him back into his own home—it continues to be his son's home as well—and there, the gift of his father's love is offered anew.

THE PARABLE OF THE UNWORTHY SERVANT (MATTHEW 18:23–35)

The first servant owes a tremendous amount of money to his master. So when his master threatens to put him into prison until he repays the entire debt, it is, effectively, a punishment and not a viable means for the master to obtain the money owed him. How can the servant earn the money in prison? He can't. That is why the master's subsequent act of simply canceling the entire debt is such an act of extraordinary grace, an act taken entirely at the master's initiative and for his own reasons. The master gives to the servant what the servant can never earn for himself: freedom, a new life. What a wonderful gift to be offered!

Tragically, this servant really doesn't "unwrap the gift." On his way from his gracious master, he encounters a fellow slave—a companion—who owes him a rather insignificant amount of money. He throws his equal into prison. Whatever the value of the wonderful gift he was offered by his master, it remained a buried treasure, an unwrapped gift. It made no difference in the way he understood himself or his companion, and it certainly was a poor way of reflecting to his master the thanksgiving and gratitude that should have helped form his life from that point on.

That this first servant does not unwrap the gift is tragic indeed. For the master, upon hearing of his actions toward the second servant, has the first servant thrown into prison. A gift unwrapped is a gift unused. And, as this parable indicates, sometimes a gift unused may be interpreted as a gift scorned.

FOR REFLECTION

1. What is your understanding of grace? What does grace allow you to do? What does it mean to "lose grace"? to "gain grace"?

2. If you were to ask various classes of grade-school children what their experiences of grace have been, what answers would you expect? (And if you did this, what answers surprised you?) How could you encourage these children to see that their lives are "graced," and that God is part of their lives even when they are not in church?

3. In the first chapter we discussed the notion that the liturgy and the sacraments are work. Part of this work is "using" the grace the sacrament offers. What, then, is the "work" of Baptism? of Reconciliation? of Confirmation? of Matrimony?

4. Continue to reflect upon the two parables that concluded and summarized this chapter. Are the experiences of any of the characters in the parables experiences you have had in dealing with family, friends, and colleagues? How could these experiences be used in helping others prepare to celebrate the sacrament of Reconciliation?

5. In the parable of the prodigal son, pay particular attention to the older son's attitude and response. Ask those to whom you minister to add a half-dozen verses of their own to this parable. How would the story end? Be sure to have them include a response from the older son, as well as a response from both his father and his younger brother.

4 The Sacraments and Their History: The Changing Ways and Means of Expressing Eternal Truths

KEY QUESTIONS

• How did the Church come to teach that there are seven sacraments? When did the Church begin to teach that there are seven sacraments?

• How has Church thinking about the sacraments changed?

• Given the historical development of the sacraments, what does it mean to say that each of the sacraments was *instituted by Christ*?

AS WE BEGIN

• When speaking of the sacramental practice of the Church, it is important to avoid two extremes. "We've *never* done it that way" and "We've *always* done it this way" are statements that will seldom, if ever, be true.

• The Church has a long and complicated history, and so

it should not be surprising that the Church's sacraments do as well. One fascinating aspect of that history is that at times secular and pragmatic reasons have contributed to the development of the pastoral practice of a sacrament as much—sometimes, perhaps more—than did prior and systematic theological reflection.

This chapter examines the historical development of the sacraments from two perspectives. First, I offer a concise overview of the historical development of each of the seven sacraments. Second, I consider the "history of our approach to and understanding of" the sacraments. Prior to this, however, let us consider the logical question: "How did there come to be seven sacraments?"

HOW MANY SACRAMENTS ARE THERE?

The official teaching of the Catholic Church, set forth by the Council of Trent in its 1547 *Decree on the Sacraments*, is that there are seven sacraments—no more, no less. But the Church has not always taught this. In fact, for the first thousand years or so of the Church's history, the answer to the question, "How many sacraments are there?" would likely be another question: "Exactly who is it you are asking?"

There is the tendency to think that the Church's teachings, Scriptures, and sacraments existed as we know them now from the very beginning. At times, some people think that any suggestion to the contrary is to challenge our belief that the Church was founded by Christ and that the bishops are the successors of the apostles. I am reminded of the old saying: "In a land where the sun is worshipped, it will surely be a crime to examine the laws of heat."

To know that there is a history to the sacraments—to examine how both the pastoral practice and the theology of the sacraments has developed over the course of time—

is to enrich our understanding and appreciation of our Church, not to threaten our belief that our Church was instituted by Christ. A study of history reminds us that our Church has a rich tradition, and that tradition is a most honorable one. For the development of sacramental theology and practice reflects a Church who has always tried to respond spiritually (and often temporally) to the different needs of different people at different times.

Not everything we associate with the Church has been there from the beginning in the form or shape we know it now. The Church, guided by the Spirit, "has gradually recognized this treasure [the sacraments]," and "has discerned over the centuries" that there are seven sacraments (*CCC*, #1117). That is why, prior to the thirteenth century, the answer to the question, "How many sacraments are there?" would depend on whom you asked—and when!

For example, Saint Augustine might have responded "two" or "three"—or he might have answered "twenty." Reflecting upon the practice of his time, Augustine would have recognized at least Baptism, the Eucharist, and Reconciliation as "especially significant visible words essential to the life of the whole Church." On the other hand, Augustine also understood sacraments in a more general sense, in keeping with his description of the sacraments as visible words.

Augustine saw many things that pointed us toward Christ and put us into contact with the divine, and these were certainly sacramental: not just Baptism, but the holy water itself; not just Reconciliation, but the ashes inaugurating the season of Lent. Augustine even considered feasts, such as Christmas, Easter, and Pentecost, as sacraments in the sense of visible words: they showed us something, told us something, and gave us some kind of experience of God. Augustine (and the early Church in general) was less interested in determining a precise number of sacraments, and more interested in helping people experience the power and grace of those things in this world that were doors to the sacred.

In fact, there are significant differences between the way the early Church and the Church of a thousand years later approached sacramental theology and practice. We consider these differences later in this chapter, including how the number of seven sacraments was determined. For now, it is necessary to clarify that when the Church did determine that the number of the sacraments was seven, that number did not come out of nowhere.

From "Sacramental Instinct" to the Recognition of a Sacrament

It is important to distinguish between what we might call the Church's *instinct* of each sacrament and the Church's *recognition* and *ratification* of these instincts as being sacraments in the strict sense. For example, there is no evidence that the Church had a formal, liturgical celebration of Reconciliation in her earliest days. Here, a historical note is necessary.

We must remember that the early Church (the first five or six centuries) had neither modern means of communication nor her present well-organized and centralized administration at her disposal. Sacramental practices—and the theologies accompanying them—could vary, depending upon which country (or which area of a country) you were in. In fact, well into the second century, many theologians throughout the Church world were discussing whether forgiveness of sins after Baptism was even possible. The earliest, comprehensive description of a process or ritual of Reconciliation comes from the treatise *On Penitence*, written by the African theologian Tertullian around the year 203.

It is equally clear, however, that the instinct behind

what would eventually become recognized and ratified as sacramental Reconciliation was there from the beginning. We only have to read Paul's First Letter and Second Letter to the Corinthians (written a mere two decades after Christ's death and resurrection) to understand that Paul saw the need for a grievous offender to be excommunicated (literally, "taken from the community"). He also saw the hopeful possibility that the offender would be "remembered" (brought back into the community) when satisfaction had been made and the sinner's repentance had been judged genuine. The same instinct can be detected behind each of the other six privileged liturgical celebrations that the Church "has discerned over the centuries . . . [as being] in the strict sense of the term, sacraments instituted by the Lord" (*CCC*, #1117).

A BRIEF HISTORY OF THE SACRAMENTS

Accounts of the historical development of the sacraments are plentiful. (One readily available study is Dr. Joseph Martos's *Doors to the Sacred*, listed in the Bibliography.) Limitations of space prevent a detailed presentation of the history of each of the sacraments. I do offer brief accounts of the historical development of each sacrament, with three goals in mind. First, I want to suggest how each sacrament has a complex history. Second, I want to suggest how practice of our sacraments today in some ways differs and in some ways is similar to the practices of the early Church. Third, I hope to whet your appetite for sacramental history, and so encourage you to pursue this study further.

Along with these three goals, I offer a caution. Volumes could be (and have been) written on the historical development of each of the sacraments. While lengthy expositions are often the enemy of the reader, brevity is often the enemy of accuracy, if not clarity. I encourage you to study the history of the sacraments in more detail than I can present here—particularly if you have the responsibility of "handing over" part of our tradition to others.

BAPTISM

The Catholic Church was not the first to use water rites in conjunction with religious or sacred celebrations. The Church gave these rites a new meaning, however. No longer was the bath seen as a repeated, ritual purification to be performed before eating or praying. Rather, being washed with this holy water was now seen as a once-and-for-all entrance into a new life of grace, a new life of participating in the death and resurrection of Christ.

Baptism is the sacrament mentioned most often in the New Testament. Although Saint Paul never describes a rite of Baptism, much of his writing—especially his letters to the Romans and the Galatians—talks of the meaning and effects of Baptism. It is likely that in the earliest days of the Church, Christians were baptized in the name of Christ. By the time Matthew's Gospel was written (about 85–90 A.D.), however, the Trinitarian formula—that which constitutes the form of the sacrament of Baptism today—was in use (see Matthew 28:19).

Adult Baptism: The celebration of adult Baptism—at first, no doubt, a simple, if solemn, immersion or pouring of water—soon evolved into a lengthy, elaborate ritual. Early Church documents describe a process of Baptism involving a catechumenate, sponsors, and anointings with oil. These documents also explain that the process of Baptism did not conclude with the actual celebration of the sacrament. Those newly baptized, now called *neophytes*, or the "newly enlightened," continued to receive instruction about their faith and their new life in Christ for some days afterward. In many places, they would return to the Church every day for a week to listen to the bishop explain more about what they had done at their Baptism and, because they were now baptized, what they would have to do in the future as Christians. Some of these post-baptismal homilies—one example is Saint Ambrose's treatise *On the Sacraments*—may be considered among the first "textbooks" of sacramental theology.

Over time the elaborate, complex process of making Christians faded from the Church's ordinary practice. There are many reasons for this, but among the more important were the rapid growth of the Church and the subsequent increase in the practice of infant Baptism. Today's Rite of Christian Initiation of Adults (RCIA) is a restoration of several components of the early Church's practice of initiating its new members.

Infant Baptism: Some scholars continue to argue whether the early Church baptized infants. Referring to the New Testament, they point out that the standard "baptismal pattern" was the proclamation of the Gospel, the personal and conscious decision to accept that proclamation, and then the voluntary submission to being baptized.

These arguments need not concern us here. The New Testament neither definitely confirms nor rules out infant Baptism as a practice in the early Church; there are, in fact, some New Testament passages that speak of households or families being baptized. At any rate, Tertullian, writing around the year 200 A.D., expresses his displeasure with the practice of baptizing infants and even young adults (a sure sign that this was a regular practice in his day). Another early third-century document, the *Apostolic Tradition*, speaks matter-of-factly about baptizing the children before the adults, and having their parents or another family member answer for them if they are unable to do so.

In the year 313 A.D., the Edict of Constantine effectively put an end to the persecution of Christians, thus making it "safe" to become one. As Christianity was declared the state religion, with Emperor Constantine himself being one of its devotees, it also became somewhat politically and socially advantageous to join the Church. As a result, the Church experienced rapid growth in its membership. At first many people became catechumens but did not go on to become baptized until later in life (Constantine himself followed this practice), since the penitential practice in many places allowed only one "forgiveness" after Baptism or imposed continued hardships upon penitents even after they had been reconciled. Clearly, these factors could only encourage one to choose carefully one's time of conversion. As time went on, however, infant Baptism became seen as more necessary, due to the development and emphasis of the doctrine of original sin. Coupled with the high mortality rate of newborns for much of humankind's history, infant Baptism had, by the eighth century, become the regular, expected, and necessary practice of sacramental initiation.

Infant Baptism continues to be the way most Catholics are brought into the Church. One irony is that, until recently, infants who were baptized were sacramentally initiated according to a rite that was a modified, child-adapted version of the rite of Baptism for adults. The Church did not have a rite of Baptism designed from scratch for infants until the publication of the 1969 *Rite of Baptism for Children* (*RBC*). Because of this, perhaps, many people continue to have a preconciliar understanding of infant Baptism. This is why the following chapter treats the "new" RBC in some detail.

CONFIRMATION

In one sense, the history of Confirmation is no more complex than that of the other sacraments. Yet, unlike the other sacraments, Confirmation seems to remain—after some twenty centuries—a sacrament "in search of a theol-

ogy," as a well-worn phrase has it. In the case of Confirmation, it is especially important to remember that the
instinct of the sacrament (if not the rite or practice) existed from the beginning. In the earliest days of the Church,
it was understood that the "giving of the Holy Spirit" was
part of what happened when one was baptized, even
though there was a great deal of discussion about exactly
how or precisely when in the rite this took place.

The "sealing with the Spirit," or the "perfecting of
Baptism," began to be known as *Confirmation* in Gaul
(modern-day France and Belgium) by at least the fifth century. By that time, the regular practice was for the bishop
to preside at this ceremony and, if a priest or deacon
presided at the Baptism because the bishop was unavailable, the Confirmation would be postponed until later.
The growth of the Church—both in population and geo-
graphically—certainly contributed to the regular post-
ponement of Confirmation; more people, particularly
infants, were being baptized—and over a greater territory.
There simply were not enough bishops available to confirm them immediately after Baptism.

The theology of Confirmation has always involved the
Spirit, certainly, but the precise understanding of the manner of the Spirit's contribution has varied. The dominant
understanding in the Scholastic era was that Confirmation
gave one the strength to become a "soldier of Christ" and
thereby a better witness to or defender of one's faith.
Aquinas distinguished the baptismal sacramental character
from that given by Confirmation by understanding the
former as a *passive power* (the power to receive the other
sacraments) and the latter as an *active power* (the power to
witness the faith in the world).

Although the Protestant Reformers rejected the idea
that Confirmation was a sacrament in the strict sense of
the term, our Church declared that there was no doubt

that Confirmation truly was a sacrament. It is obvious, however, from the variety of ages at which it is administered today, that there is some doubt about Confirmation's "proper" or most appropriate theology: whether it is, in actual practice, a sacrament of initiation, or whether it is, in practice, an opportunity for those baptized as infants to confirm their now adult or adolescent faith.

In our Western Church, Confirmation ordinarily is conferred along with Baptism only when an infant or young child is in danger of immediate death or, more frequently, it is conferred on non-baptized adults who are brought into the Church during the Easter Vigil. The Eastern Churches have maintained the unified celebration of Baptism, Confirmation, and Eucharist, even for infants.

EUCHARIST

Obviously, the celebration of the Eucharist was present from the very beginning of the Church's history. It was the Eucharist that made the Church; it was the Eucharist that called Christians together to celebrate the Lord's passion, death, and resurrection, and his continued presence in the lives of believers.

The earliest scriptural witness to this is Saint Paul's description of the Last Supper in 1 Corinthians 11:23–25, written less than a generation after Jesus shared the Last Supper with his disciples. What we know today as the Eucharist probably had its most basic origins in the weekly meal of fellowship Jesus celebrated with his disciples and friends, a meal intrinsic to the Jewish observance of the weekly Sabbath. After Jesus' death and resurrection, the disciples and others continued these meals—although, of course, their understanding of that Last Supper with Jesus changed forever the significance of their gathering.

Paul's First Letter to the Corinthians describes a

Eucharist that is still celebrated in conjunction with the supper of fellowship. As time went on, however, the focus became more on what we know now as the Eucharist, and so the fellowship meal became separated from the Mass. One reason for this was likely the problem Paul reports:

> When you come together, it is not really to eat the Lord's supper. For when the time comes to eat, each of you goes ahead with your own supper, and one goes hungry and another becomes drunk. (1 Corinthians 11:20–21)

Those concerned with current liturgical abuses can take heart that, in the words of the Old Testament writer Qoheleth, "there is nothing new under the sun" (Ecclesiastes 1:9). The earliest account we have of the Christian Eucharist is also the earliest account of eucharistic misuse and abuse.

By the middle of the second century, the basic structure of the Eucharist as we know it today was in place, as is seen by my summary of Chapter 67 of Saint Justin Martyr's (d. 165) *Apology I*, written around the year 150:

> We gather on Sunday. The lector reads from the accounts of the apostles or from the writings of the prophets for as long a time as we have available. After this, the president encourages us through his sermon to follow the good example we have heard about. Then we stand and pray.
>
> After this, bread, wine, and water are brought to the table. The president prays and gives thanks. . . .
>
> The gifts over which the thanksgiving has been spoken are distributed, and deacons take them to our absent brothers and sisters. Those who can contribute their money to the president do

so; he uses it to provide for those in need.

This basic structure of the eucharistic celebration remains with us, although the ritual of celebration became much more elaborate over the centuries. The books by Johannes H. Emminghaus and Lawrence J. Johnson, listed in the Bibliography, detail the history and development of the Mass in general and of the individual elements of our eucharistic celebration.

RECONCILIATION

As mentioned above, the instinct of Reconciliation is evident in Paul's two letters to the Corinthian community. The earliest discussions dealt with whether those who had been baptized (especially adults) could be readmitted into the community if they had sinned grievously (e.g., murder, idolatry, apostasy). Once that question was answered in the affirmative around the mid-to-late second century, the question then turned to how many times this post-baptismal forgiveness was possible.

The African theologian Tertullian wrote *On Penitence* around the year 200 A.D., and his treatise tells us several things about the Church's sacrament of forgiveness at that time. He mentions that a ritual of "contrition, confession, and absolution" had developed; that the Church considered no sin as unforgivable; and that the community was actively involved in the process of Reconciliation by their prayers and intercessions. As time went on, the process of Reconciliation developed until it became almost a kind of second catechumenate—and in fact, some writers (Tertullian being one of them) referred to Reconciliation as a "second Baptism."

The lengthy penitential process and the order of penitents remained on the books for several centuries, but it was practiced less frequently as time went on—and as the Church continued to grow in numbers. The penances assigned were often long and severe, and many times, even after the penitent was brought back into the Church, some hardships remained—such as not being able to have sexual relations with one's spouse, or not being able to return to a particular career. The long and arduous penitential process worked well for a heroic Church—a Church in which a conscious, lengthy, deliberate discernment by both individual and Church was required for admittance (as witnessed by the prebaptismal catechumenate). As more infants were brought into the Church through Baptism, however, belonging to the Church began to be more a "fact of life" for many Christians than a thought-provoking and life-shaping commitment.

Reconciliation as we know it today—the private encounter between a penitent and a priest, with penance given after the celebration of the sacrament—had its origins in the spiritual direction between monks and lay people in the Celtic islands when the missionaries began preaching there in the sixth century. By the eleventh century, the order of penitents was extinct in practice if not also in theory. Throughout the next few centuries, the sacramental practice of private, repeated "Confession" developed, and received more than adequate support from the people's practice and the theologians' treatises.

ANOINTING OF THE SICK

The Letter of James, written sometime after the year 90 A.D., offers evidence in its fifth chapter that prayers and an anointing with oil were a special act of the Church for its sick members. Documentary evidence suggests that, in the very early Church, all Christians could anoint the sick as long as they used oil that had been blessed by the bishop. A practice from the beginning, Anointing was first referred to as a "kind of sacrament" by Pope Innocent I in the year 416. This reference elevated its dignity as a formal and special action of the Church and, unfortunately, initiated its slow evolution from an anointing of the sick to an anointing of the dying (Extreme Unction). Although the early practice of this sacrament dealt with the healing of the *person* (physical recovery was by no means ruled out), the effect of the sacrament eventually came to be considered as a rescuing of the person's *soul*. At least one prominent thirteenth-century theologian even suggested that the best time to anoint persons was when they were nearly dead; that way, there would be little chance of recovery and, therefore, little opportunity for further sin.

The Anointing of the Sick is an excellent example of a sacrament whose theology and practice changed tremendously in the first thousand years of the Church's history—and whose theology and practice has changed tremendously again within just the last twenty-five years. Until the postconciliar reform of the sacrament, the practice was to administer Extreme Unction near or at the point of death, and the theology complemented the practice. The matter and the form, the "core statement" of what the purpose of the sacrament is, left no doubt that this sacrament prepared one for heaven. The matter of the sacrament was the anointing of the head and each of the person's senses (eyes, ears, nose, hands, etc.), while the formula accompanying the anointing asked God to forgive the person "whatever sins have been committed through the sense of sight, hearing, smell, touching, etc."

The postconciliar practice and theology of the sacrament is far different. The sacrament is again called the Anointing of the Sick, for it is for a person who "begins to be in danger due to sickness or old age" (*Code of Canon Law*, #1004–§1). And, as it did in the past, the proper matter and form today reflect the theology of the sacrament today. (Recall from Table One in Appendix I that the forehead and hands—representing the whole person—are anointed. Furthermore, the sacramental formula is again "comprehensive," speaking more of the whole person, rather than focusing primarily on the spiritual effect of the forgiveness of sins.)

HOLY ORDERS

The word "priest" is found in the New Testament only in the Letter to the Hebrews, and there it refers to the Eternal Priest, Jesus Christ. It is clear, however, that the Church had designated leaders from its beginning. The Pastoral Epistles (the letter to Titus and the two letters to Timothy) speak of a handing over of the tradition to worthy people, people who will preserve and safeguard that tradition, and who will preach as much by their example as by their words.

Before the end of the first century, the offices of bishop (elder-presbyter) and deacon had developed and were seen as constituting a line of succession and authority from the apostles. Scholars continue to debate exactly when and how these men became associated with presiding over the eucharistic celebrations of their communities (and, in the case of the apostles, whether they did). As early as the end of the first century, Saint Ignatius of Antioch makes it clear that only the bishop or his direct designee enjoys this privilege. By the end of the second century, the three-fold division of ordained ministry into bishops, priests, and deacons seems prevalent throughout the Church.

From Hippolytus's *Apostolic Tradition*, written in the year 215, we know that, by that time, a rite of ordination had developed to the extent that priests were ordained by the bishop and by other priests laying their hands on them. Once ordained, these priests ordinarily concelebrated the Eucharist with the bishop, although with his permission they could preside if the bishop was unavailable.

The status, prestige, and authority of bishops and

priests began to increase after Christianity became the official religion of the state in the fourth century. Much of the development of the priesthood follows the development of the Church: priests became co-workers with the bishops, especially in the larger cities and in the more rural areas where the bishops and their principal assistants, the deacons, could not meet all the needs of the people.

The development of the priesthood certainly follows the development of the celebration of the Eucharist as well. By the time of the Protestant Reformation in the mid-sixteenth century, priestly identity was focused primarily on the priest's sacramental ministry. For centuries it was understood (though never solemnly defined by the Church) that the matter for the sacrament of Holy Orders was the handing over of the chalice and paten to the new priest, because these core "visible words" seemed to express best the essence of priesthood. Significantly, in the year 1947 Pope Pius XII stated that the matter of Holy Orders was to be understood as the bishop's imposition of hands over the priest—thus signifying clearly that ordination was the consecration of the whole person for a life of holiness and service to the Church, and not simply the assigning of and empowering for specific sacramental duties.

MATRIMONY

Of the seven sacraments, Matrimony was the last to be recognized by the Church and proclaimed a sacrament on par with the other six. There are several reasons for this. Some theologians found it difficult to find in the Scriptures a clear "institution" of this sacrament by Christ, as they did for the other sacraments. For others, the fact that marriage involved sex presented at least theoretical difficulties to Matrimony being considered a sacrament. Given Augustine's teaching that sexual intercourse even within marriage was almost always at least a venial sin, it was difficult to understand how something involving sex could be an instrument of grace—an essential component in defining what a sacrament did and, therefore, what could be considered a sacrament.

There was no "sacrament" of Matrimony between Christians in the early Church. A second-century letter tells us that "Christians do not differ from other men and women in country or language or customs. . . . They marry like everyone else." Nevertheless, the instinct that the marriage of Christians was in some way different from those of non-Christians is found in 1 Corinthians 7. Also, Saint Ignatius of Antioch (d. ca. 107) advised Christians to consult with their bishop before marrying, so that their marriage would be "in accordance with the Lord and not on account of passion."

It does not seem as though liturgical blessings or ministerial participation in marriage existed before the fourth century. When the Church did begin to become actively involved in the celebration of marriage, that involvement was due to both the Church's growing influence in the secular world and, related to this, the Church's assuming many of the duties and responsibilities for the organized operation of society. Apparently there was no liturgical rite of Matrimony mandatory until after the time of Charlemagne (ninth century), although by four hundred years later, sacramental rites of Matrimony—and the understanding of Matrimony as a sacrament—were becoming rather well established.

Our century has witnessed a remarkable shift in the understanding of sacramental Matrimony, the primary development being the move away from seeing the marriage relationship as a *contract* and understanding it more in terms of the biblical notion of *covenant*.

FROM RECOGNITION TO RATIFICATION: AND THEN THERE WERE SEVEN

As we move into the third millennium, it is interesting to note that the first few centuries of the second millennium set a "tone" that continues to influence our approach to sacramental theology even to our day. As the world emerged from the Dark Ages, knowledge and scientific interest experienced a rebirth. Universities were founded, serious studies marked every branch of education, and theology itself became known as the "Queen of the Sciences."

In the preceding two chapters we introduced various technical terms: for example, *ex opere operato*, *matter*, and *form*. Much of this technical language owes its existence to the scientific approach to theological reflection that dominated the eleventh through the fourteenth centuries. While this "scientific, theological" approach contributed greatly to the development of many sacramental concepts and teachings, it also encouraged a more analytical and less experiential approach to the sacraments.

Why are there seven sacraments? The short answer is: the Church teaches that there are seven sacraments. The long answer is: by the time theologians in the eleventh century and thereafter began to adopt a more systematic approach to sacramental theology, seven liturgical actions had attained a premier status (again, each of the instincts behind these liturgical actions was founded upon Christ's life).

Theologian Peter Lombard (d. 1160) made an important contribution to the notion that there are seven sacraments. In his *Sentences*, a collection of opinions ("sentences") from various theologians on various topics, Lombard listed what we know today as the seven sacraments; he considered them to be privileged liturgical rituals that met the definitional requirements for a sacrament ("a visible sign instituted by Christ to give grace"). Lombard was neither the first nor the only theologian who offered definitions or counted numbers in those days, but he was one of the more influential. In the following century, Thomas Aquinas relied upon Lombard's writings, and contributed to their influence by suggesting that it made sense that the sacraments were seven in number.

In question number sixty-five in the third part of his *Summa Theologica*, Aquinas reasoned that the spiritual life has a "certain conformity" with the life of the body. Baptism, then, was spiritual birth, Confirmation was growth in the Spirit, and the Eucharist was nourishment for the soul: three sacraments that responded to the spiritual life just as birth, an increase in size and strength, and food were part of "growing up" in the physical life. Thomas went on to say that Reconciliation (reflecting the practice of the day, he called it "Penance") and Anointing of the Sick (Extreme Unction) corresponded to the need for physical healing, while the sacraments of Holy Orders and Matrimony met the spiritual needs corresponding to society's needs for regulation and propagation.

Important Church councils over the next few centuries (Lyons, 1274; Florence, 1439) supported Lombard's and Aquinas's teachings. When the number seven was challenged by the Protestant Reformers in the sixteenth century, the number seven was established by the Council of Trent in 1547.

Adding to the "long answer" as to why there are seven sacraments, we note that the number seven is theologically attractive in another way: it is one of the highly symbolic numbers often used in the Bible to denote fullness or completion. God created the world in seven days, for example, and there are seven gifts of the Holy Spirit. That there are seven sacraments suggests that the grace of Christ, through the actions of his Church, envelops all of humankind and our needs.

I conclude this discussion by relating an anecdote that allows me to make two additional points. Not long ago, I read a "letter to the editor" in a national weekly Catholic newspaper. The writer found it obvious that the Church's understanding of the sacraments was seriously flawed because childbirth, an event that in her opinion surely brought grace, was not considered on par with "the seven." If my interpretation of her comments is correct, she suggested that if the Church were to raise childbirth to the status of an official sacrament, such a decision would, among other things, enhance the dignity of women.

My first point is that the Church is not going to "change" the number of the sacraments. That number has been decided—defined—by the Council of Trent. What that definition of Trent does not mean, however, is that the sacraments are the only ways by which and through which we can receive or experience God's grace. We live in a world of symbols, and we live in relationship with others. We can experience God's grace—God's communication to us, and the effect of that communication—through these symbols and through our relationships. Hopefully, we do experience God's grace there!

When Trent declared that there are seven sacraments, the Council in no way intended to suggest that God's grace is bound or limited to the sacraments. To affirm this would be to suggest that the Church has control over the grace of God—an assertion that an accurate understanding of the sacramental teaching of the Church would refute definitely and definitively.

My second point is that it would be easy to turn the question of "how many sacraments *should* there be?" into a kind of Catholic parlor game. In some ways, such a discussion might be of some use, in that it might allow us a better understanding of the many ways God can and does act in the world and in our lives. But allow me to change the question: why did God send Jesus to institute seven sacraments? *God didn't.* God sent Jesus to *be* the great sacrament of God's love for humankind. The seven sacraments of our Church are among the most important times and the most significant ways in which we can see and experience clearly what God did for us in Christ. How was Jesus the great sacrament of God? How is the Church the fundamental sacrament of Christ? Those are questions well worth asking.

AN OVERVIEW OF THE "ATTITUDE" OF SACRAMENTAL THEOLOGY

As we have seen, each of the seven sacraments has its own history, and each sacrament experienced numerous changes throughout the centuries. Furthermore, as the practice of the individual sacraments changed, so did the Church's way of understanding what the sacraments did—and, in fact, what the sacraments were. Theology influences and informs how we celebrate the sacraments ("we do what we believe"), but history also tells us that at times changes in the practice of a sacrament came before the theological reflection that would express the new practices.

For the purposes of our overview, we will consider two thousand years of Church history. Looking at the first millennium, we would characterize the first five hundred years or so as a time of rich development and elaboration. During these centuries, the Church was growing rapidly in number and developing its sacramental rituals. The practices surrounding the celebration of Baptism and Reconciliation are particularly illustrative examples of the Church's changing sacramental practices which led to a changing "attitude" toward the sacraments.

FROM PUBLIC AND COMMUNAL TO PRIVATE AND INDIVIDUAL CELEBRATION

In the early Church—here we are talking about the third through the fifth centuries—Baptism and Reconciliation were public, communal affairs. Adults being baptized engaged in a lengthy catechumenate, and the community regularly prayed for and over them. The community also assigned them sponsors to assist in their conversion and to testify their good intentions to the local Church. As we indicated earlier, Baptism, conducted ordinarily during the Solemn Easter Vigil, consisted of a complex series of rites and, for at least the first week after they were baptized, the new Christians continued to come together as a group for further instruction in their new faith.

Similarly, Reconciliation was a public and communal affair and, in many ways, the order of penitents resembled the order of catechumens. While penitents would not confess their sins before all, they performed many acts of penance in the presence of the community they had offended. The community supported them by good example and prayers, and the penitents were reconciled, often on Holy Thursday, in a public ritual officially "re-membering" them—bringing them back into the Church. The importance (and we might say, the necessity) of the community's involvement is seen clearly in Tertullian's *On Penitence*, an early third-century document that contains a wealth of information about the practice and theology of early Church penitential discipline. Addressing the penitents, Tertullian writes:

> Where there are two together, there is the
> Church—and the Church is Christ. When,
> therefore, you stretch forth your hands to the
> knees of the brethren, you are in touch with
> Christ and you win the favor of Christ by your
> supplications. In like manner, when they shed

tears for you, it is Christ who suffers, Christ
who supplicates the Father. And what the Son
requests is always easily obtained.

This notion that the community, as well as the "minister" and the "recipient," were actively and effectively
involved in the celebration of Baptism and Eucharist (and
the other sacraments) had long disappeared by the time
the Scholastic theologians began compiling their systematic treatises on the sacraments. Like most theologians,
these men based much of their analysis of the sacraments
on their own experience of celebrating the sacraments, and
the celebration of Baptism and Reconciliation had become
far more private and less elaborate than in the Church's
early years. The community was certainly not actively
involved in the actual process of Reconciliation; it was
"celebrated" with as much secrecy as possible. Infant Baptism was not celebrated in secret, but the emphasis and
tone of the rite suggested that it was more an urgent, family affair than it was a congregation celebrating the initiation of a new member.

FROM LEARNING *THROUGH* THE SACRAMENTS TO LEARNING *ABOUT* THEM

A similar radical difference may be observed when we consider how people learned about the sacraments. In the
early Church (especially in the grand, solemn liturgies of
the third through the fifth centuries), it is no exaggeration
to say that people learned the meaning of the sacraments
by celebrating them. For it was in the celebration that the
people would experience for themselves what the effects of
the sacraments were. The postbaptismal catechesis offered
to the newly baptized by Saint Ambrose and others, in
fact, encouraged the neophytes to think back to what actually happened during the ceremony: to remember how
they felt physically as they were immersed into water and

anointed with oil, stripped of their old garments and clothed in the new—and to consider that what they felt "on the outside" symbolized what was taking place "on the inside." Here, Baptism was clearly a "visible word," a word that was not merely spoken and heard, but was seen and experienced as well.

Regarding the process of Reconciliation, it is clear that those in the order of penitents experienced penance. They were separated from their fellow parishioners, and were sometimes forbidden even to enter the church. They fasted and often dressed in sackcloth and ashes. Imagine how they felt when finally they were led back into their church and reconciled by the bishop imposing his hands upon them in the presence of their community.

But by the time Aquinas and his fellow Scholastic theologians began to write their theology, the practice of both sacraments was much different—as was the experience. The urgency of baptizing infants was so emphasized that rituals of that era even called for the child to be baptized without the mother being there, if her postdelivery recovery would unduly prolong the time of the Baptism. As for Reconciliation, "Confession" was an apt term for the practice at that time. Even when those approaching the sacrament were guilty of the most grave sins, the order of penitents had been telescoped into a private encounter between priest and penitent, in which the confession of sins, the offering of counsel, the assignment of a penance, and the words of absolution ordinarily took only a few minutes.

These differences in sacramental practice extended to the way in which people learned about the sacraments— and to what they learned. Most adults, having been baptized as infants, would have no recollection of their own Baptism. Their experience of the sacrament was standing off to the side at the Baptism of their own newborn son or daughter, while the priest interrogated the infant through the godparents. Ordinarily only a few friends or other family members would be present for the ceremony. The notion that Baptism incorporated their child into a community was "known" more from its being taught than from it being experienced. There was nothing in the rite that spoke of a conversion experience—appropriate, since it was an infant that was being baptized. The significant change that Baptism effected was a change that, again, was taught more than experienced: through the waters of Baptism, original sin was remitted and the gates of heaven were now open to the infant.

Similarly, preparing for Reconciliation primarily consisted of receiving instruction as to how to make a "good confession." Sacramental catechesis would talk about grace, conversion, and the need for forgiveness, but it would emphasize "confessional techniques": what sins had to be confessed, how they were to be confessed, and what procedure had to be followed if the penitent had forgotten to mention a specific sin. The priest was certainly seen as a minister of the Church, but in the minds of most, he represented God more than he did the Church. This was not surprising, since sin was understood more as an offense against God—or at least as a matter between God and penitent alone. There was little in the celebration to suggest or encourage the experience of being brought back into the community one had offended by sinning.

FROM LIVING *LIFE NOW* TO PREPARING FOR A HEAVENLY *LIFE LATER*

Perhaps the greatest difference between the "sacramental attitude" of the first and second millennium is the understanding of why it was important to celebrate the sacraments in the first place. The third, fourth, and fifth centuries are often considered the "golden age" of the

Church's liturgical practice, and the celebration of the sacraments of Baptism and Reconciliation contributed in no small way to this thinking.

When one was baptized, it was clear that one was entering a community of people here on this earth whose life had been changed because of Christ. These people were considered the saints on earth. They had their eyes on heaven, but they were conscious that their Baptism oriented them—bound them—to live their lives in this world in a most unworldly way. Baptism didn't open the gates of a future heaven, as a later age would put it, as much as it showed the way to heaven through this life. The same may be said for Reconciliation. The offender to whom Paul refers in his First Letter to the Corinthians was excommunicated because he had gone against the community's way of life on this earth (see 5:1–5). Two centuries later, as we have seen, Tertullian stressed that a person who sins offends the community as well as God, and so needs to obtain forgiveness from both.

A thousand years later, however, much of this thinking had changed because the experience of celebrating the sacraments had changed. In the popular understanding, infant Baptism was more a priest's act that made heaven possible, and less a community's action of initiating a new member. The motive for Confession was primarily to prevent an individual from dying in a state of mortal sin and therefore having to spend eternity in hell; less was considered and taught about how our celebration of the sacrament should improve the quality of our community's life here on earth.

The chart at the end of this chapter summarizes these changes in the Church's approach to the sacraments. It is a generalization—a caricature, if you will—of two very different approaches to the sacraments at two very different times in the history of the Church and of the world. As a generalization, it should be used with the appropriate caution. It is considered as one of the points in the Chapter Summary.

We have examined the history of the sacraments in general, and have also considered the history of the Church's "attitude" toward the sacraments. The following two chapters consider the two primary sacraments of the Church: Baptism, the "gateway to life in the Spirit," and the Eucharist, the "source and summit of ecclesial life."

CHAPTER SUMMARY

CHANGES IN THE CHURCH'S APPROACH TO THE SACRAMENTS

Examples: Baptism, Reconciliation	Third, fourth, and fifth centuries	Thirteenth, fourteenth, and fifteenth centuries
WHO Who are the main "participants" in the sacramental celebration?	The bishop (priest), the candidate, the community	The priest and the parishioner
HOW How is the meaning of the sacrament learned by the people?	By participating in and experiencing the action of the sacrament	Instruction; catechism
WHY Why is it necessary to celebrate the sacraments?	So that we might better live our lives now for the good of the Church, the Body of Christ on Earth	So we will be able to enter heaven after death
HOW LONG How long does it ordinarily take to celebrate this sacrament?	Baptism and Reconciliation both involve a lengthy process, a public "ordo"	Baptism and Reconciliation take "no time at all," and are seldom seen or understood as "communal" actions

1. Each of the seven sacraments has a complex history. In this case, "a little knowledge can be a dangerous thing." DREs responsible for teaching the history of the sacraments should study the history of the sacraments in more detail than has been presented here.

2. Although the Church did not definitively set the number of the sacraments as seven until the sixteenth century, the instinct underlying each of the sacraments was present from the beginning.

3. Ultimately, Christ did not come "to institute seven sacraments." Christ came to *be the sacrament* of God's love for humankind.

4. A major thrust of postconciliar theology is to recover and restore some of the early Church's understanding of and attitude toward the sacraments: that they are celebrations of the community; that they are to be experienced and not merely performed; and that they point first to the way we should live our lives now.

FOR REFLECTION

1. An official, solemn teaching of the Catholic Church is that Christ instituted the seven sacraments. Given the complex history of the sacraments, how can we explain that the Church, from the beginning, had seven sacraments?

2. From the brief histories of the sacraments offered here, what aspects of their celebration seem familiar to our practice and experience today? What aspects seem foreign?

3. How was—how is—Christ the fundamental sacrament of God's love for us?

5 The Sacrament of Baptism: The Gateway to Life in the Spirit

KEY QUESTIONS

• What are the religious and ecclesial (personal and communal) effects of Baptism?

• How does the RCIA speak to the importance of Baptism? What are the fundamental theological principles upon which the RCIA is built? What is the basic structure and process of the RCIA?

• How is the Church's "new" RBC different, theologically and pastorally, from its predecessor?

• How do the theologies of the Baptism of adults and of children complement each other?

AS WE BEGIN

• Vatican Council II's *Sacrosanctum Concilium* (*SC*; *The Constitution on the Sacred Liturgy*) called for the appropriate revision of the sacramental rites so that they would "be given new vigor to meet present-day circumstances and needs" (#4). Speaking specifically of the Baptism of adults, *SC* said: "The catechumenate for adults, comprising several distinct steps, is to be restored . . . By this means the time of the catechumenate, which is intended as a period of suitable instruction, may be sanctified by sacred rites to be celebrated at successive intervals of time" (#64). The new rite of Baptism for adults is the *RCIA*, published first in 1972.

• Concerning the Baptism of children, *SC* stated: "The rite for the baptism of infants is to be revised, its revision taking into account the fact that those to be baptized are infants. The roles of parents and godparents, and also their duties, should be brought out more clearly in the rite itself" (#67). The new *RBC* was among the first of the Church's sacramental rituals to be revised following the Council; it was published first in 1969.

Baptism, the first sacrament that all Christians celebrate—indeed, the sacrament that "makes us Christian"—merits a chapter of its own in our study. We examine Baptism from three perspectives. First, we consider the sacrament in general, and look at some of the theological principles that support our understanding and practice of the sacrament. The second and third perspectives examine, respectively, specifics pertaining to the Baptism of adults and of infants.

Some DREs may not be involved directly in their parish's RCIA process, or in preparing parents for the Baptism of their children. The principles and the process guiding the RCIA are important to understand, however, for they address what it means to live, pray, and work as a Christian community. Regarding the Baptism of infants, many DREs were so baptized, as were the majority of children and young adults with whom they work. The more we understand our Baptism, the more we will understand and appreciate the sacraments we subsequently celebrate.

BAPTISM IS THE DOOR TO LIFE IN THE SPIRIT

As we discussed in the previous chapter, there is no doubt that the Church initiated new members through the baptismal waters from the very beginning. Baptism is the sacrament most often mentioned in the New Testament and, although Saint Paul never describes an actual rite of Baptism, it is clear that this sacrament is fundamental to his understanding of the Christian's life in Christ.

BAPTISM IS A GREAT GIFT

In Chapter 3, we observed that a sacrament confers two things upon those who celebrate: the religious reality, or grace; and the ecclesial, or "Church," reality that, in the case of Baptism, is referred to as the "sacramental character." Let us consider each of these two effects of Baptism.

As for its religious or spiritual effects, the two principal meanings of Baptism—the forgiveness of our sins and our new birth in the Holy Spirit—are expressed well by the visible words of the sacramental rite: the pouring with, or immersion into, water. But Baptism has other meanings as well, and there are many images that explain the gifts Baptism confers. Baptism is a rebirth, a cleansing, the making of a new person; it is our adoption, our consecration, and the receiving of our inheritance.

So great is the power of this sacrament that not only are all sins (original and personal) forgiven but, in the case of adults, all punishment due to all personal sins is remitted. This is to be "born again" indeed! And this is to be "adopted": to be taken out of one's unfortunate situation and placed in the more favorable existence we call the life of grace. Rebirth and adoption are but two of the many images the RCIA and RBC draw upon in expressing the meanings of Baptism. Table Two in Appendix I provides a convenient reference to the location of these and other images in the adult and infant rites, as well as a list of relevant passages from the Scriptures and the *CCC*.

What Baptism does not do—and, sadly, we know this only too well from our experience—is take away our tendency or inclination to sin. Sin remains a real possibility for baptized Christians, because sin—one definition of which is "doing our own will"—remains attractive. Our tendency to allow our lives to be distracted and distorted by the lure of sin is what our Catholic tradition calls *concupiscence*. Concupiscence often is thought of as referring to lustful temptations, but it really refers to all those tendencies—envy, pride, anger, excessive living—that "encourage" us to be less than the persons we are called to be.

As we have mentioned, Baptism is one of three sacraments that, once validly celebrated, cannot be repeated. Along with Confirmation and Holy Orders, Baptism confers, in addition to grace, a sacramental character. This indelible spiritual mark configures us to Christ and marks us as "belonging to him." Through Baptism we become Christ's property! As Saint Paul reminds us in his letter to the Romans:

> We do not live to ourselves, and we do not die to ourselves. If we live, we live to the Lord, and if we die, we die to the Lord; so then, whether we live or whether we die, we are the Lord's.
> (Romans 14:7–8)

As the parable of the prodigal son suggests (see our discussion in Chapter 3), we may lose the grace of Baptism by sinning, but our identity as a child of God, given us through our Baptism, cannot be lost.

Baptism confers upon us the grace of justification and, through the baptismal character, we are given a certain visible status in our Church. (See *CCC*, #1266 for further explanation of the "grace of justification.") As the introduction to both the adult and infant rites of Baptism makes clear, through Baptism we are incorporated—brought—into Christ and the Church. And as is the case with the sacramental character conferred through Confirmation and Holy Orders, status in the Church means service in and for the Church.

Baptism Is a Great Burden

Baptism gives us status in the Church. But if status means service, then Baptism is a burden as well as a gift. This thought should not surprise us, for it has a history almost as old as the sacrament itself. In his treatise *On Baptism*, written around the year 200 A.D., Tertullian remarked that those who truly understood what Baptism asked of them would "have more fear of obtaining it than of postponing it."

Baptism is a burden because to be baptized is to be committed to following Christ. Baptism is a burden because it is the "gateway to the spiritual life," the door to the other sacraments which, as we have discussed, are not merely actions performed in church, but are also orientations and guidelines for living as Church. As we have said, the liturgy and the sacraments—Baptism—are work. Baptism is a process, not an accomplishment, and if Baptism does offer the gift of the remission of all sins and their punishments, it also confers upon the baptized the responsibility to live and act in response to that grace. This "burden of Baptism" is described well by understanding Baptism as a "change of ownership and allegiance" on our part; we are still servants and slaves, but to God, not to sin (see Table Two, Appendix I).

If Baptism places a burden upon us, it also gives us the spiritual strength and resources to bear the burden. We find a subtle hint of this in the opening chapters of each of the three synoptic Gospels (Mark, Matthew, and Luke). As he is baptized by John in the Jordan River, Jesus is identified by God as his Son, and he receives the Holy Spirit. What happens next is, to say the least, unexpected. Immediately after he is baptized, Jesus goes out into the desert to be tempted. In fact, all three Gospel writers make it clear that it is the Spirit who leads Jesus into the desert to be tempted. (Mark even says the Spirit "drove him out.") It is clear that, even for Jesus, being baptized and so identified as God's Son does not remove the trials and difficulties of being obedient to God's will.

What is equally clear from these accounts, however, is that the Spirit who descends upon Jesus at his baptism and leads him out into the wilderness is the same Spirit who gives him the grace—the orientation, the strength—to remain faithful to his identity as God's Son. Using Matthew's Gospel (4:1–11) as our guide (and adding a few of my own words for clarification and emphasis), we can see how and why Jesus turned away from the sinful attractions offered him:

• Satan: (You have been fasting forty days . . .) "*If* you are the Son of God, command these stones to become loaves of bread."

Jesus: (I *am* God's Son, and so I live . . .) "One does not live by bread alone, but by every word that comes from the mouth of God."

• Satan: "*If* you are the Son of God, throw yourself down [from the top of the temple]; for it is written, 'He will command his angels concerning you.'"

Jesus: (I *am* God's Son; you may tempt me but . . .) "Do not put the Lord your God to the test."

- Satan: "All these [kingdoms] I will give you, *if* you will fall down and worship *me*."

  Jesus: (I am *God's* Son, and so . . .) "Worship the Lord your God, and serve *only him*."

The burden of Baptism is that it places us in the service of Christ. The gift of Baptism is that it is *his* service to which we are committed, and so it is his grace and protection that we receive. We will continue to discuss the gift and burden of Baptism, but let us now do so in the context of the rites of adult and infant Baptism.

THE BAPTISM OF ADULTS IN THE POSTCONCILIAR CHURCH

Jesuit priest Francis J. Buckley once led his readers down a fantasy trip based upon an imagined discovery of an ancient manuscript containing a fragment from the Acts of the Apostles:

> Then Philip began to speak, and starting with this scripture, he proclaimed to him the Good News about Jesus. As they were going along the road, they came to some water; and the eunuch said, 'Look, here is water! What is to prevent me from being baptized?' 'Nothing,' said Philip, 'except paragraphs 7, 20, 21, 34 and 36 of the *Rite of Christian Initiation of Adults*.' ("The Right to the Sacraments of Initiation." *Origins* [November 9, 1978]: p.329)

Father Buckley's pointed humor comments appropriately on the "baptismal mood" of the American Catholic Church in the postconciliar years. The Second Vatican Council's *SC* called for the appropriate revision of the sacramental rites. Anyone who thought these revisions would consist primarily of subtle changes in wording or the rearrangement of minor details of celebration would have been surprised by the complex ordo known as the RCIA. With the publication of the RCIA, the Baptism of adults in the Catholic Church would never be the same.

Nor would the Baptism of infants or children—for the serious approach to Baptism promoted by the RCIA influenced our approach to infant Baptism as well. "Anonymous parishioners" who showed up in the pastor's study to arrange for the Baptism of their infant child might hear none of the expected congratulations, but rather, a number of pointed questions about what evidence they could offer indicating their genuine intentions to raise their child in the Catholic faith. For reasons such as this, Father Aidan Kavanagh, O.S.B., the foremost American authority on the RCIA, once described the adult ordo as the "most explosive pastoral document to be issued since the council." In his view, the RCIA was not simply a new rite for baptizing adults; it was an ordo that offered "a radical renewal for the whole of Christian life."

While the RCIA certainly will not solve all the Church's problems and difficulties, many believe it would be difficult to overstate its importance. The principles upon which the RCIA is built are important not only for our understanding of Baptism but also for our understanding of what it means to act as Church. Let us consider briefly three of these principles.

• *"Christians are not born, they are made"*: This oft-cited phrase comes from Tertullian, and his words stress that becoming a Christian is not something that just happens. Baptism, like liturgy, is *work*: it is the Christian's employment, the Christian's vocation. The celebration of Baptism, then, is not a ritual performed in a few moments of time (or, as is the case with the RCIA, after a lengthy catechumenate), but is a ritual that effects and signifies one's incorporation into Christ and the Church and thus commits one to living in Christ and the Church. To be baptized is not to have accomplished something; it is to have begun to live a life in and for Christ, in and for the Church. That Baptism is a process of initiation is reflected clearly in the rites of the RCIA, which we will consider below.

• *Sacramental initiation is a process that affects—and effects—the whole community*: The Church is not divided into "those who are baptized" and those who are "about to be." Two traditional descriptions of our Church are that it is "always reforming, always in need of reform," and "always reconciling, always in need of reconciliation." The same reciprocal relationship may be applied to initiation. Our Church is a Church that must always be initiating new members, and it is a Church that must be continually reinitiating itself into the mystery of Christ it celebrates. By bringing in new members, the Church engages in a never-ending process of continuing education and formation as to what it is about—and why.

• *Becoming a Catholic involves more than learning "facts"*: Catechesis is an integral part of the RCIA, and it is clear that catechesis involves more than the learning of Church doctrines, history, and personalities. These are important things to learn, to be sure; Catholics should know, for example, a good part of what is presented in this booklet. Ultimately, however, catechesis is not about mastering facts, but about embracing a way of life: a way of life built upon and nourished by liturgy, common prayer, spirituality, and apostolic works. Learning how the Church is Church is as important as learning what the Church is.

Postconciliar theology stresses that we must take the Church seriously. The postconciliar rites of initiation tell us that if we are to take the Church seriously, we must take Baptism seriously. Obviously, the RCIA takes both Church and Baptism seriously. Let us now briefly consider the adult rite of Baptism.

THE STRUCTURE AND PROCESS OF THE ADULT RITE OF BAPTISM

The RCIA is composed of four distinct stages, each having its own focus, goals, and liturgical rites that reflect and support those goals. There is no shortage of commentaries upon or resources for understanding and implementing the RCIA. Table Three in Appendix I provides a convenient outline of the ritual structure of the RCIA, and can be used to guide one through the comprehensive rite itself (readily obtainable in most parish offices). To supplement the table, I offer three comments.

First, catechesis proper to each stage is essential. Again, catechesis of the Catholic faith ultimately is instruction in embracing a Catholic way of life, and so deals with more than the imparting of Church "facts" and teachings. The teachings must not be ignored, however. Preparing for sacramental initiation into the Church is radically different than applying for membership in a private club. Actions do speak louder than words, but the actions of the Church are supported by and related to specific beliefs, convictions, and teachings of the Church.

Second, with the exception of the third stage (the period of purification and enlightenment, which takes place during Lent) the length of each stage of the RCIA process is and should be flexible. In practice, it seems that the second stage, the catechumenate, often begins with the school year and is necessarily seen as having to end as the third stage begins with Lent. While it is true that none of us would ever receive any of the sacraments if we waited until we were perfectly ready or perfectly prepared, it must be emphasized that the process of the RCIA cannot be strictly regulated and should certainly not be rushed. How long should each stage last? The ideal answer is: as long as it needs to, as long as it takes to meet the "conversion goals" of each stage.

Third, it seems that the most neglected stage of the RCIA in many parishes is the fourth stage, the period of mystagogy, or postbaptismal catechesis. Baptism is the beginning of one's life in Christ and his Church, not the culmination of that life. DREs may be particularly influential here: on-going catechesis, postbaptismal catechesis, is important for both the newly baptized and the parish. The Church continues to initiate itself by continuing to reflect upon the death and resurrection of Christ, the central mystery of our faith. An ideal time to focus this reflection is the time set aside for the mystagogy: the eight-week period beginning with Easter and concluding with Pentecost. Post-baptismal catechesis—for those just baptized *and* for Catholics of many years standing—should be a regular feature of a parish's liturgical life throughout the Easter season.

THE BAPTISM OF INFANTS IN THE POSTCONCILIAR CHURCH

DREs likely will not be involved in the actual celebration of infant Baptism. Some, however, may help with programs that prepare parents for the Baptism of their child, while others may be called upon to explain why "this family's baby" is being baptized at "my Sunday Mass!" Furthermore, the majority of children and young adults with whom DREs work will have been baptized as infants. It is important, therefore, to look at infant Baptism in some depth. Subsequent preparation for celebrating the sacraments of Reconciliation and Confirmation would do well to emphasize that, since we are receiving these additional sacraments because we have been baptized, exactly what does our Baptism mean? What did it do for us?

WE BAPTIZE INFANTS OUT OF HOPE, NOT FEAR

Many Catholics believe the primary reason for baptizing

infants is to free the child from original sin—that sin by which Adam:

> . . . as the first man, lost the original holiness and justice he had received from God, not only for himself but for all human beings. (*CCC*, #416)

Growing up in a parochial grade school in the late 1950s and early 1960s, I was taught that a child dying without Baptism would spend eternity in limbo—a kind of "border-line state" in which no pain would be experienced, but neither would the full joy of heaven and the beatific vision.

Most theologians today consider the concept of limbo as itself being in limbo. It was a once popular theological opinion that tried to address the "discrepancy" between how a merciful God could keep a baby out of heaven, and the Church's teaching that Baptism is necessary for salvation. Limbo has never been a Church teaching; rather, it was a hypothesis, a conjecture, of some theologians.

Those charged with easing parental concerns and presenting Church teaching faithfully will find a valuable resource in the *CCC*, which offers a calm and reasoned hope.

> As regards *children who have died without Baptism*, the Church can only entrust them to the mercy of God, as she does in her funeral rites for them. . . . All the more urgent is the Church's call not to prevent little children coming to Christ through the gift of holy Baptism. (#1261)

Original Sin Is Real; Fortunately, Grace Is More Powerful

To maintain that limbo (or the fear of it) has no place in the theology or practice of infant Baptism is to deny neither the doctrine nor the reality of original sin. Even a casual rubbing of shoulders with those around us furnishes abundant proof that original sin is alive and well. Nor does discounting limbo as the "state" of unbaptized infants dilute the teaching that Baptism is necessary for salvation. Baptism is necessary for salvation because grace is necessary for salvation. For it is grace—grace made possible by Jesus' redemptive suffering and death on the cross; grace offered to us through the loving initiative of God—that allows us to be born again at the font, and that sustains children, adolescents, and adults day after day on that continuing journey of conversion we call Christian life.

Baptism is for Christians the ordinary (which does not mean "simple" or "routine") means by which the extraordinary gift of grace is conferred and celebrated. And it is God's grace—never limited to ordinary means—that we need, for we cannot "purchase" for ourselves the redemption purchased for us by the inestimable cost of the cross. God's gift of grace is necessary for our salvation, and Baptism is the ordinary means through which this extraordinary gift is effected, sacramentalized, and celebrated for infants of Catholic parents.

There Is a Limbo We Should Be Concerned About

The link between infant Baptism and original sin should not be theological speculation as to how God can receive unbaptized infants, but rather the pastoral application of how the Christian community can receive infants in such a way that they will learn, from the beginning, the community's ways and means of overcoming the effects of original sin that linger stubbornly in the lives of all. Baptism is the pledge and promise that infants are delivered from original sin—not by slow trickles of water, but by the flood of grace that rushes forth as they are transformed and brought into the family of God and the Church. Infant Baptism does not mean that the children are "home free," but that they are brought into a home—brought into a

Christian environment—in which the Word of God is proclaimed by word and deed from the beginning. Children learn how to be part of the family by being part of the family. Infant Baptism proclaims how infants are to live and be formed. If there is a state of limbo that needs to be addressed in our baptismal catechesis, it is not a hypothetical limbo between earth and heaven, but the spiritual limbo existing in quite tangible form in far too many homes today.

A New Rite of Baptism for Children

As we have mentioned, before the revision of the sacramental rites called for by the Second Vatican Council, infants were baptized according to an adapted form of the rite originally intended for the Baptism of adults. One of the general directives the Council stated was that:

> The rite for the baptism of infants is to be revised, its revision taking into account the fact that those to be baptized are infants. The roles of parents and godparents, and also their duties, should be brought out more clearly in the rite itself. (*SC*, #67)

The revisers of the rite took the Council's directives to heart, and there are several major differences in the "new" Rite of Baptism for Children (RBC). Questions and answers play as important a part in the postconciliar celebration of infant Baptism as they did in the preconciliar rite. Who answers the questions and for whom the answers are given, however, are markedly different.

In the preconciliar rite, the priest addressed questions directly to infants and, as they obviously could not speak for themselves, their godparents answered on their behalf. Now it is the parents who are questioned and, furthermore, the parents speak for themselves. In this way, the postconciliar RBC restores to the parents a pride in their place in the celebration of their infants' Baptism by underscoring the essential role given these "first teachers of their children in the ways of faith" (*RBC*, #70). The postconciliar RBC also sees the grace and effects of the sacrament as continuing in the home-life and upbringing of the child (see *RBC*, #3). Infants receive grace through their Baptism, but it is their parents (and their community) who receive the responsibility for nurturing that grace. As the RCIA suggests, the catechumenate never really ends, for faith must continue to be guided and nourished.

That the celebration of infant Baptism testifies to the parents' commitment to their faith is witnessed further by the relocation of a familiar phrase in one of the directives of the preconciliar rite. According to preconciliar liturgical rules, an infant was to be baptized *quam primum* (as soon as possible)—a wise directive in a baptismal ethos influenced by fears of an untimely death and doubts as to the child's eternal fate. While the postconciliar rite retains the phrase, it places it in an entirely different context. Now it is not the infant who is to be brought to the font as soon as possible, but the parents who are to present themselves to the pastor *quam primum*, so that preparation for the baptism of their child might begin (preparation which, as the RBC suggests, might take place even before the child is born).

CHRISTIAN PARENTS ARE MINISTERS TO THEIR CHILDREN

Much has been written about the family being the "domestic church." In line with this, perhaps we can do more to emphasize the ministerial role of parents within the home. A good part of that ministry, of course, is the faith formation and education called for by the RBC, and in this way parents are ministers of Christian education.

But another ministry to which Christian parents are called, and one emphasized far too infrequently, is the leading of the prayer or "liturgy" of family life. The prayer of the domestic church can certainly find regular expression at meals and upon awakening and retiring, but these are only some of the opportunities of presiding at prayer of which parents may avail themselves.

One resource helpful in this regard is the *Book of Blessings* (The Liturgical Press, 1989) which, in addition to offering blessings for use before and after a child's birth or baptism (itself, one means of spiritually preparing the family for the celebration of the sacrament), suggests numerous blessings oriented specifically toward family life. Many of these may easily be adapted so that the parents preside, and in fact the *Order for the Blessing of Sons and Daughters* is designed with the understanding that parents often "wish to bestow [the] blessing of the Lord on their own children." Encouraging a more frequent use of such resources might assist pastoral ministers in their efforts to suggest that a sacrament is not something that happens only in church and in a few moments' time. It also gives pastoral ministers an opportunity to emphasize that, as the family is the domestic church, so are the parents her primary ministers. (The National Conference of Catholic Bishops' pastoral message, *Follow the Way of Love*, is a resource helpful for promoting the idea of the sacramentality of family life.)

ADULT BAPTISM AND INFANT BAPTISM

To speak of adult Baptism is to speak of a long, guided, and thoughtful process. The RCIA speaks of maturity, decision making, and commitment: appropriate and attractive adult characteristics for our adult world. In many ways the adult ordo reflects the very best of what it means to be a disciple, to follow Christ.

By contrast, that infants "do nothing" when they are baptized quietly proclaims the unique significance of infant Baptism and a fundamental truth about all our sacraments. For the very nature and circumstances of infant Baptism point unmistakably to that which alone makes possible and gives meaning to any sacramental celebration: that God takes the initiative in dealing with us, and that it is God's offering of grace that precedes, sustains, and perseveres beyond each and every response on our part.

This consideration of God's initiative does not exhaust the theology or celebration of the sacraments, but gives due consideration—first consideration—to the source and end of theology, sacraments, and liturgy: God's initiative, God's graciousness, God's action and grace. Infant Baptism signals the fundamental truth about all our sacraments, a truth we so often and easily leave behind at the font as we enter the church to celebrate our adult liturgies or as we go about the business of our adult lives. Infant Baptism reminds us that "in the beginning there was God," that this God knew us in the womb, and that even adults who come to the faith come because God's word has called them.

As infants are brought to the font, so too are adults brought to the faith—or better, the faith is brought to them—long before they recognize their need for it or are willing to accept the demands it will make upon their lives. Notwithstanding the commendable postconciliar emphasis on Baptism as a "sacrament of faith" (and the splendid reinforcement given this emphasis by the adult ordo), we must keep sight of the fact that faith, before all else, is gift. Conversion is the turning around of our life and the profession of our faith. But it is also standing still and remaining quiet long enough so that we may realize where we already are and where we already belong because we have already been claimed. For those of us baptized as infants, the grace of our continuing conversion as adults is our constant return to the grace first offered us in Baptism, the grace to know who we are and to whom we belong.

We should feel no sacramental embarrassment or discomfort, then, when considering the "passivity" of our infants at their Baptism—nor should we stuff adult words into their mouths, as did the preconciliar rite. As the Church baptizes her infants, it is the adults who should be reduced to silence. It is the strong and the wise, the committed and the mature, the experienced and the competent, who should feel the loss for words. For in infant Baptism—as in the initiation of adults, the forgiving of sins, or the Anointing of the Sick—it is God's word and grace that effects, transforms, reconciles, and comforts.

Our response to and cooperation with this grace, our "unwrapping the gift" that is offered to us, certainly must be invited and promoted in our prayers and liturgies. But the nature and circumstances of infant Baptism challenge the adult Church to remember that God does not wait until we are ready and willing to hear God's word before speaking that word to us (as the sending of The Word clearly indicates). While we are dependent upon that word, God's free offering is not conditioned by our ability to respond. For even as adults turn to God in their times of need, they really turn themselves so that they might see he whom the prodigal son saw when he "came to himself"—his father already at the door, patiently awaiting his return, patiently awaiting his child to return to the grace he has offered him with a father's love from the beginning (see Luke 15:11–32).

The Baptism of adults and infants is one sacrament, but each emphasizes a different truth essential to our understanding of the whole sacramental economy. Adult Baptism reminds us that we must be willing, conscious, deliberate Christians. Infant Baptism asks us to recall that God not only has the last word in our lives but also—and always—the first word as well. To put it another way: a sudden explosion of grace radically changed the nature of Paul's approach to life and the Christian Church. But God's grace also builds upon nature quietly, calmly, and without fanfare. That is no less impressive—and remains for the Church just as challenging a prospect.

The sacrament of Baptism begins the life-long process of Christian initiation: a process of incorporation into Christ and his Church that is both "completed," and yet sustained and nourished, by the sacrament of the Lord's Supper. It is the Eucharist, which the Second Vatican Council's *Dogmatic Constitution on the Church* (*Lumen Gentium*) called the "source and summit of the Christian life" (#11), to which we now turn.

CHAPTER SUMMARY

1. Baptism is "the basis of the whole Christian life, the gateway to life in the Spirit, . . . and the door which gives access to the other sacraments" (*CCC*, #1213).

2. The two principal effects of Baptism are purification from sins and new birth in the Holy Spirit. Other images that express the meaning of Baptism include adoption, a change of allegiance, a new creation.

3. Baptism confers grace and a sacramental character. Grace gives one life in Christ, and the character confers upon one a certain status in the Church. This status is for service.

4. Taking the Church seriously means taking Baptism seriously. Taking Baptism seriously means understanding Baptism as a process, not an accomplishment. The

"work" of Baptism only begins at the font.

5. In both the celebration of adult and infant Baptism, it is "adult faith"—the faith of the catechumen, the faith of the infant's parents—that is questioned, challenged, and hopefully, strengthened.

FOR REFLECTION

1. What does it mean to say that Baptism is a "burden"? How can Baptism be a "gift" and a "burden" at the same time?

2. How does the Church "reinitiate" herself when she initiates new members? How does the RCIA support Tertullian's claim that "Christians are not born, they are made"?

3. How is the role of parents different in the new, postconciliar RBC? In what ways can we encourage parents to see themselves—and to act—as Christian ministers to their children? How might a baptismal preparation program for parents look if it took as one of its key themes, "Making a Family, Making the Domestic Church"?

4. How can we consider infant Baptism a paradigm for what happens in every sacramental celebration? What can the Baptism of infants tell us about adult faith?

5. The *General Directory for Catechesis* says that the catechumenate, the second stage of the RCIA process, is the paradigm for all catechesis (#88). How would you use the principles and the process of the catechumenate as a model or guide for your work in preparing others for the sacraments of Reconciliation, First Communion, and Confirmation?

6 The Eucharist: Source and Summit of Ecclesial Life

KEY QUESTIONS

• The Eucharist is the "source and summit of ecclesial life" (*Standards*, #532.303). How does the Eucharist "surpass" the other sacraments of our Church?

• The Church uses many names to refer to the Eucharist. What does each of these names tell us about this "perfect sacrament"?

• When compared with the accounts of the Last Supper found in the Gospels of Mark, Matthew, and Luke, what is distinctive about the Last Supper account in the Gospel of John?

• What is the relationship between our communal celebration of the Eucharist and private Eucharistic adoration and devotion?

AS WE BEGIN

• *Sacrosanctum Concilium* (*SC*)affirms the real presence of Christ in the Eucharist. Noting that Christ is "especially present" under the eucharistic elements, it also speaks of the presence of Christ in three other modes of expression: in the Word of the Scriptures; in the person of the minister, the priest; and in those assembled for the celebration (see #7).

• "The mode of Christ's presence under the Eucharistic species is unique. . . . 'the body and blood, together with the soul and divinity, of our Lord Jesus Christ and, therefore, *the whole Christ is truly, really, and substantially* contained.' 'This presence is called "real"—by which is not intended to exclude the other types of presence as if they could not be "real" too, but because it is presence in the fullest sense: that is to say, it is a *substantial* presence by which Christ, God and man, makes himself wholly and entirely present'" (*CCC* #1374).

The limitations of space prevent us from examining in detail the historical development of the Eucharist. These same limitations prevent us from discussing the individual elements of the Mass (the Liturgy of the Word, the Liturgy of the Eucharist). Both discussions would be valuable—and so books such as those by Johannes Emminghaus and Lawrence Johnson, listed and annotated in the Bibliography, are necessary companions to both this chapter and the *CCC*'s section on the Eucharist (see #1322–1419).

In this chapter, I first review the Church's basic teachings concerning the Eucharist. Second, I attempt to relate the theology of the Eucharist to pastoral practice. Third, I explore the relationship between our public celebration of the Eucharist and the practice of devotion to and adoration of the reserved Eucharist.

THE EUCHARIST: SACRAMENT OF "PERFECTION"

The Eucharist may be considered the "sacrament of perfection" in two ways. First, it is the sacrament that completes Christian initiation. This is especially clear in the RCIA, when adults are baptized, confirmed, and then communicated at the Easter Vigil. It is, unfortunately, less clear when, as is the situation in many dioceses, children receive their First Communion—the completion of Christian initiation—some years *before* receiving yet another sacrament of initiation, Confirmation.

Second, the Eucharist may be considered a "sacrament of perfection" in that it is "the source and summit of the Christian life" (*Standards*, #532.303):

> The other sacraments, and indeed all ecclesiastical ministries and works of the apostolate are bound up with the Eucharist and are directed towards it. For in the most blessed Eucharist is contained the whole spiritual good of the Church, namely Christ himself our Pasch . . . (Second Vatican Council, *Presbyterorum ordinis*, 1965, #5)

While all the sacraments make the truth more real to us, the Eucharist contains, in a special way, he who is our Way, our Life, and our Truth. The visible words—the matter and form—of the Eucharist are not anointings of oil that call to mind Christ's ministry to the sick, or prayers asking God to be gracious; the matter is bread and wine which becomes Christ himself, and the words of the sacramental form are the words of Christ himself at the Last Supper. The Eucharist is the sacrament of our Church; it is the sacrament that *makes* the Church. The Eucharist is the sacrament we, literally, "take and eat"; it becomes a part of us so that we might become more like the One we receive. As the priest prays at the preparation of the gifts, pouring a few drops of water into the wine:

> By the mystery of this water and wine may we come to share in the divinity of Christ, who humbled himself to share in our humanity.

MANY NAMES, MANY TREASURES

In biblical language, to know someone's name is to have a

certain power over them. To know a person's name is to know something about that person's essence, about his or her identity. One's name is considered an essential part of one's identity, which is why we often see a person's name being changed in Scripture when that person's relationship with God changes. God changes Abram's name to Abraham, for example, when God "commissions" him to be the father of many nations. Jesus changes Simon's name to Peter when he calls Peter to follow him and become a fisher of people. Saul becomes Paul when he meets the Lord God on his way to Damascus—and when his life is changed forever.

It is most appropriate that the Eucharist, the "perfect sacrament," goes by various names, for no one name says it all. The richness of this sacrament is inexhaustible—no one name totally captures its meaning—and so many names are needed. Each name tells us a part of the mystery we celebrate and are called to enter into fully.

The *CCC* offers nine names (and a brief commentary) for the Eucharist, each of which refers to a particular part of the hidden treasure this sacrament offers us (see #1328–1332). One sentence, however, combines several of these names or concepts, and reminds us that, while we "work" at celebrating the Eucharist, this "perfect sacrament" is first of all the work of the Trinity:

We must therefore consider the Eucharist as:

- thanksgiving and praise to the *Father*;

- the sacrificial memorial of *Christ* and his Body;

- the presence of Christ by the power of his word and of his *Spirit*. (#1358)

Thanksgiving to the Father; the sacrificial memorial of Christ; the work of the Spirit: let us briefly consider each of these definitions or descriptions of the Eucharist.

Thanksgiving and Praise to the *Father*

The fundamental name of this sacrament that is the source
and summit of ecclesial life is *Eucharist*. The Greek word
from which *Eucharist* is derived expresses well both the
central action of our celebration and the reason why we
celebrate. When we gather as Church, we "do
Eucharist"—we "give thanks"—for God's actions on our
behalf in the past, for his presence among us now, and for
his promise that he will remain with us in the future.

While the Eucharist is primarily an act of thanksgiving
for God's work in Christ, we also give thanks for the
whole of God's creation. This is expressed most often in
the various prefaces by which we begin the Eucharistic
Prayer. These prefaces thank God for his work throughout the history of the salvation of humankind, sometimes
by referring to specific actions of God, other times (for
example in the prefaces for the feasts or memorials of
saints) by reminding us how God has worked in and
through the lives of others.

To celebrate the Eucharist is to embrace a spirit of
thanksgiving, the basic attitude of Christians. As we mentioned in Chapter 1, a weekday preface expresses this well:
"You have no need of our praise, yet our desire to thank you
is itself your gift" (*Sacramentary*, Preface for Weekdays IV).

The Sacrificial Memorial of *Christ* and His Body

"Memorial" does not simply mean a passive remembering
of events that have taken place in the past. The Eucharist
is a memorial in the sense that it is an active proclamation,
the continuing announcement of who we are because of
what God has done for us through his Son. This memorial
is also a proclamation of the good news that Jesus does
change our lives.

The "sacrificial" aspect of the Eucharist as memorial

must not be overlooked, for it is the sacrifice of Jesus on the cross that gives the Eucharist its abiding power in our lives. The Last Supper is not just one of many meals Jesus shares with his disciples. At this meal, Jesus shares himself in a special way—a way that will forever change his disciples' understanding of him, of themselves, and of their mission (see *CCC*, #1365).

The Presence of Christ by the Power of His Word and of His Spirit

It is through the words of Christ himself and the power of the Holy Spirit that the bread and wine we offer are offered back to us as Christ's Body and Blood. Just as each of the Eucharistic Prayers contains the *words of institution*—those words Christ said at the Last Supper that identify the bread and wine as his Body and Blood— so are those words preceded in each Eucharistic Prayer by the *epiclesis*, the calling upon the Spirit to:

> . . . make these gifts holy, so that they will become for us the Body and Blood of our Lord Jesus Christ. (Eucharistic Prayer II)

THE EUCHARIST IN PRACTICE: CULT AND CONTROVERSY

Discussions about the Eucharist often seem to take on a life of their own. Almost a generation ago, the American liturgist Nathan Mitchell entitled his fine study on the worship of the Eucharist outside Mass *Cult and Controversy*—a title that aptly describes just about any discussion of any aspect of the Eucharist we might have anytime, anywhere, with anyone. The source and summit of the Church's life and activity seems to invite as much controversy as it does attract "cult" or worship.

To take one example: anyone who recently built or

renovated a church knows that the question of "where the Blessed Sacrament is to be reserved" is seldom a simple, pragmatic inquiry into physical location or aesthetic considerations. One answers this question carefully, because one's answer (it is claimed) will reveal much: from how one understands the meaning of the eucharistic celebration to—in the minds of some—even whether one really believes in the real presence.

Discussions about the Eucharist often take on a life of their own—and often distract us from taking on the life the Eucharist offers us. It is this life, and the demands the Eucharist makes upon our life, that I address here. Put another way, I do not intend to assess the theological complexities of transubstantiation or to resolve the real meaning of real presence. (Still less do I want to discuss the location of the tabernacle!) My interest here is in what I consider, ultimately, a more difficult question: "Because we celebrate the Eucharist, because we have the Eucharist, *who are we?* Who *must* we be?"

We should define the Eucharist with all the theological acumen and precision we can muster. But we must also ask: "*How does the Eucharist define us?*" I offer three points for further reflection.

TRANSUBSTANTIATION: MORE THAN A CHANGE IN BREAD AND WINE

The Council of Trent considered transubstantiation a "fitting and proper" explanation of how the whole substance of bread and wine is changed into the substance of the Body and Blood of Christ. Trent's definition is requisite for the Catholic teaching and understanding of the real presence.

While the *CCC* clearly affirms the true, real, and substantial presence of Christ under the signs that express and communicate his love for us (see #1373–1381), it also concedes that this real presence of Christ can be apprehended, ultimately, only by faith. Referring to the words of Saint Cyril of Alexandria, the *CCC* encourages us:

> 'Do not doubt whether this is true, but rather receive the words of the Savior in faith, for since he is the truth, he cannot lie'. (#1381, quoting *In Lucam* #22, #19)

But the Eucharist is not only about the changing of bread and wine into the Body and Blood of Christ. The Eucharist is that, to be sure, but it is more. The "why" of transubstantiation—the truth transubstantiation tries to make more real to us—only begins to be revealed when bread and wine become the Body and Blood of Christ. Transubstantiation speaks of a change in the gifts we place upon our altars so that our lives may be transformed, so that we might become more like the One we receive ("May he make us an everlasting gift to you," in the words of Eucharistic Prayer III).

If these reciprocal changes—the change in bread and wine, the changing of our lives—seem unrelated to us, then we still have not heard those compelling words that Matthew's Gospel offers us about our worship of Christ in the Eucharist. There we are told that if we remember someone has something against us even as we bring our gift to the altar, we are to leave our gift and first attend to them (see 5:24). Clearly we are to seek peace with each other as we worship the Prince of Peace; we are to make communion before we receive Communion.

Love God *and* love your neighbor. These commands are joined, not because they are different sides of the same coin, but because they are the only side of the one currency that allows us entrance into the Kingdom.

"Do This in Memory of Me"—But What Is "This"?

The New Testament offers us five accounts of the Last Supper Jesus has with his disciples. For our purposes we consider four of these accounts—those in the Gospels of Mark, Matthew, and Luke, and the one in Paul's First Letter to the Corinthians—as of one piece. Differences notwithstanding, we are told that Jesus takes bread and wine, says the blessing, identifies the bread and wine as his Body and Blood, and tells the disciples to "do this in memory of me."

We find something much different, however, in the account of the Last Supper that the Gospel of John offers us. Of all the Gospel writers, only John has no words of institution over the bread and wine—perhaps, in part, because by the time this last of the canonical Gospels was written, there is little need to remind Christians that Jesus identifies the bread and wine with his Body and Blood.

But what John does find necessary to include (was it already in danger of being forgotten?) is the command that the disciples wash each other's feet.

> 'So if I, your Lord and Teacher, have washed
> your feet, you also ought to wash one another's
> feet. For I have set you an example, that you
> also should do as I have done to you.'
> (13:14–15)

Jesus' instruction to "do this"—spoken not of the offering of bread and wine at the table, but of humble service to one another in daily life—seems the necessary consequence to the identification of the bread and wine with the Body and Blood of Christ in the Synoptics. Indeed, several generations before John's Gospel, Paul senses this unbreakable connection (and is, perhaps, the first Christian to speak of the location of tabernacles) for he charges, "Do you not know that you are God's temple and that

God's Spirit dwells in you?" (1 Corinthians 3:16).

The Eucharist is not celebrated and then "cleaned up and put away." What's more, adoration of the Blessed Sacrament misses the mark if our private devotion bears no public fruit. Leave it to crusty Saint Paul. Only he can get away with suggesting that if we cannot genuflect figuratively (serve humbly) before the image of God in our brothers and sisters, then we cannot—without guile, without hypocrisy, without presumption—even consider genuflecting literally before Christ under the appearances of bread and wine.

THE EUCHARISTIC SACRIFICE NEEDS TO BE CELEBRATED REPEATEDLY—BECAUSE THERE IS ALWAYS SOMETHING IN US THAT IS LACKING

It seems that many Catholics today are uncomfortable talking about the Eucharist as a sacrifice. Sacrifice speaks too much, they claim, of violence or injustice, of poverty and death. Far better, it is thought, to describe the Eucharist with words warm and life-giving, words of sharing, of eating and drinking, of storytelling, and of missioning.

But the language of sacrifice is not about injustice or violence; it is about mercy and peace. And Christian sacrifice speaks not about poverty and death but, ultimately, about richness and life. Here, the etymology of the word itself is instructive. To *sacrifice* is *sacrum facere*: "to make holy, to do the holy." Thus Christian sacrifice is not about giving something up or forfeiting something of great value. Rather, it is about "making holy," "doing what is holy," and thus receiving more because we have become more.

Furthermore, discussions as to how our sacrifice at the altar is the repetition (or re-iteration or re-presentation) of the sacrifice on Calvary Hill are pointless, unless we realize that we need to regularly celebrate the Eucharist.

There are things we need to do and say often in our lives or, otherwise, we risk forgetting who we are and why we are here.

The sacrifice of Christians is not an act of self-praise. Nor do Christians offer sacrifice to appease an angry God. Christian sacrifice is neither narcissistic nor fatalistic, but eucharistic. And doing Eucharist—giving thanks—is one act Christians must do time and again. For to give thanks is to acknowledge that we are in debt *because we have been graced*.

As the German theologian Hans Urs von Balthasar once shrewdly observed, it is the Christian religion, communicated by the eternal child of God, that constantly reminds its believers that *they* are children—and that, therefore, they must ask and give thanks for things: not because the gifts would be refused, but precisely so they may be recognized as gifts.

EUCHARISTIC ADORATION AND DEVOTION

As mentioned above, the phrase "cult and controversy" seems an apt way to describe many discussions concerning the Eucharist. Perhaps this is seen nowhere more clearly than in many unfortunate discussions that begin with making a distinction between the "static presence" of Christ in the Blessed Sacrament and his "dynamic presence" in the eucharistic celebration—and then end up in trying to make it a case of one or the other.

To practice devotion to the Blessed Sacrament is to know that, historically, the practice of reserving the Blessed Sacrament originally developed as a way to assure that the Eucharist as Viaticum would be available for the dying, and that extra hosts would be available for the celebration of the Eucharist when necessary. Historical facts are just that, however; they tell us something about the past, without automatically suggesting the present or dictating the future.

History suggests that devotion to the reserved Eucharist began to play an increasingly important part in Catholic spirituality in the tenth and eleventh centuries. Exposition of the Blessed Sacrament arose partly (perhaps in large part) as a response to those who denied the real presence of Christ in the Eucharist. Devotion to the reserved Eucharist was encouraged because many people felt unworthy to approach the communion rail and literally take the Body and Blood of Christ within them. Devotion to the Eucharist developed, then—at least in part—as responses and countermeasures to eucharistic controversies and to the people's perception that they were unworthy to receive Communion.

I suggest that our eucharistic controversies have yet to be entirely resolved. We may not deny the real presence of Christ in the Eucharist, but I respectfully suggest that many of us have a long way to go in affirming, in appropriating, what that real presence means for us. As we discussed in Chapter 1, *liturgy* comes from the Greek words that mean "the work of the people." And, as we have and will continue to stress throughout this booklet, we must "work" at the sacraments: assume the responsibility the gift gives us, as well as accept the grace the sacrament offers.

There are times when it is necessary to "do the work" so the Lord may be served and praised. But, as the story of Martha and Mary (see Luke 10:38–42) makes clear, there are times when we must set aside our work—even the important "work" that our liturgy is—to hear the Lord speak to us in the way that he can only when the language we use is not the spoken, sung, audible language of public ritual, but the quiet language of one heart alone with its greatest love—and with its greatest lover. I suggest that if we do not spend time alone with the Lord whose presence we celebrate at Eucharist, then our own eucharistic controversy continues, for we will not discover, we will not experience, how real and personal the Lord's presence can be.

Certainly, we would not want to return to the days when our unworthiness before God was repeatedly shoved in our face. We gather around the table to celebrate the Eucharist because we can boast in the Lord, as Saint Paul says, and because we are called to sing a joyful song, as the psalmist says. But just as Christians are not those who pray *either* alone *or* with others, neither are Christians those who either *do* ministry or *receive* it from others. Following the Lord's example, we pray together *and* alone; we give *and* we receive.

We must not allow our sense of unworthiness to keep us away from the celebration of the Lord's table. But we should allow our sense of unworthiness to bring us before the Lord, face-to-face, one-on-one, in the absolute "noisy silence" of our hearts. Some things can be heard only in silence. If "the life of prayer is the habit of being in the presence of the thrice-holy God and in communion with him" (*CCC*, #2565), some parts of that life can only "happen"—can only be initiated, developed, and strengthened—at those times when we deliberately suspend our work and our words and let God speak to us. Although the just-cited quotes appear in the *CCC*'s fourth section ("Christian Prayer"), they are not unrelated to our discussion here. The context of the image of "thirst" is that of John, Chapter 4—Jesus' encounter with the Samaritan woman at the well (see *CCC*, #2560).

The Eucharist is the source and summit of the Church's activity. Yet how often we hear from others—how often we ourselves feel—that our experience at this life-giving table is uneventful, routine, even boring. We know the difficulty. "How can we revitalize our eucharistic celebrations?" is a topic discussed at countless meetings, seminars, and planning sessions. Allow me, perhaps, to begin some "eucharistic controversy" here. I suggest that if we know and experience Christ only in the "active celebration of the Eucharist"—if we know him only when *we* "call him down," only when *we* proclaim the readings, sing *our* songs, and offer *our* gifts—I suggest that if these are the only times we know Christ, then perhaps we do not know him *on his terms at all*. Certainly we must know Christ at the eucharistic table, but we must know that Christ's presence, before all else, does not depend upon what *we* do. First, and last, Christ's presence among us—Christ's presence in our lives—is grace. And, as Saint Paul says, it is by this grace that we are saved, not by anything we have done—not even by the great work that the liturgy is (see Ephesians 1:5–14). Rather, we are saved because of what Christ has done for us (see Titus 3:5).

I have suggested that how we define the sacraments (and the Eucharist) is less important than how the sacraments define us. Discussions about the real presence cannot absent us from showing that the Christ of the Gospels continues to make a real difference in our lives. Arguments about the location of tabernacles in our churches are resolved to no end if we do not look for the image of God in those around us. And the definitions of the mysteries of our faith that discipline our theological thinking remain sterile intellectual exercises unless we allow those mysteries to discipline and define us and how we act.

The ultimate power of the sacraments is not their ability to change the way we think about our faith, but their ability to change our lives. Likewise, the Eucharist will never be the Word made flesh for the world by attaching doctrines, dogmas, and teachings to it—but only by showing the world the difference it continues to make in us.

Baptism incorporates us into Christ and his Church, and the Eucharist is the source and summit of the

Church's life. As we know, our Catholic Church recognizes five additional sacraments. Each of these furthers our identity as God's adopted sons and daughters; each of these nourishes and supports our life in Christ's Church. In the next chapter, we will discuss the significance of the sacraments of Reconciliation, Anointing of the Sick, Matrimony, Holy Orders, and Confirmation.

CHAPTER SUMMARY

1. The sacrament of the Eucharist completes Christian initiation. The Eucharist is the "perfect" sacrament: it is "the source and summit of the Christian life" (*Standards*, #532.303).

2. Eucharist, the Lord's Supper, the breaking of bread, the eucharistic assembly, the sacrificial memorial: no one name captures completely the mystery and the power of this sacrament through which Christ gives himself to his Church for all time.

3. *The* Christian attitude is thanksgiving. *The* Christian sacrament is the Eucharist. We give thanks for God's work on our behalf in the past, for the sacrifice of God's Son, Jesus Christ, and for the continuing presence of God and his Son in our lives and in our Church through the working of their Holy Spirit.

4. The Church teaches that transubstantiation—a change of the whole substance of the bread and wine into the substance of the Body and Blood of Christ—is a "proper and fitting" way to understand the "real presence" of Christ under the appearances of the sacramental elements. The Church recognizes also that this mystery can be best approached, ultimately, by faith.

5. "Do this in memory of me." This command of Jesus refers to the taking, blessing, and giving of the bread and wine that is his Body and Blood. It refers also to Jesus' command to his disciples in John's account of the Last Supper, to "wash one another's feet" (13:14). What we receive in the Eucharist we must not keep to ourselves.

FOR REFLECTION

1. The *CCC* offers nine names for the Eucharist (see #1328–1332), each of which suggests a part of this great act of thanksgiving for God's love. Which names are most significant for you?

2. Why do we consider the Eucharist "the perfect sacrament"?

3. "You have no need of our praise, yet our desire to thank you is itself your gift (*Sacramentary*, Preface for Weekdays IV)." What does this mean? Do you agree that "thanksgiving" is *the* Christian attitude? What other attitudes support and encourage us to "give thanks," to *be* "eucharistic people"?

4. What does it mean to say that Christ is present under the appearances of: bread and wine, the gathered assembly, the Scriptures, and the person of the priest?

5. What can our celebration of the Eucharist as Church teach us about our life as Church and our life with God? What can our private devotion of the Blessed Sacrament teach us?

6. How can our parish programs and processes move from a focus on preparing to "*receive* the Eucharist" to a focus on preparing to "*live* the Eucharist"?

7 Exploring More Hidden Treasures

KEY QUESTIONS

• Is there really anything "new" about the sacrament of Reconciliation, other than its change of name from "Penance" or "Confession"?

• What is the theology of the sacrament of the Anointing of the Sick? Is this a sacrament for the dying or for the sick? And, if for the sick, for what kind of sickness?

• What is the difference in essence—not just in "degree"—between the ministerial priesthood and the priesthood of all the faithful?

• How has the Church's understanding of the sacrament of Matrimony changed in the postconciliar era?

• What is the theology of the sacrament of Confirmation?

AS WE BEGIN

• In 1614, furthering the work begun a half-century earlier by the Council of Trent, the *Roman Ritual* was published. This book contained the rites of all the Church's sacraments and, with the exception of a few minor changes, provided the pattern for the Church's sacramental practice for well over the next three hundred and fifty years. The first of the postconciliar revisions of the sacramental rites were the *Rite of Baptism for Children* and the *Rite of Matrimony*, both published first in 1969. Since then, all of the sacramental rites have undergone at least one revision.

• Of the five sacraments we consider in this chapter, the Anointing of the Sick has perhaps undergone the most radical change and development in its suggested pastoral practice. And, without much doubt, the theological understanding and pastoral practice of the sacrament of Confirmation continues to perplex us the most.

In the Introduction, I stated that just as the Council of Trent taught that not all the sacraments were of equal importance to our salvation, so too are all of the sacraments not of equal importance to DREs in their professional work. Because of this, the majority of this booklet has been devoted to understanding the liturgy and the sacraments in general, and the primary sacraments of Baptism and Eucharist. This chapter discusses the remaining five sacraments of our Church, with special attention given to the sacraments of Reconciliation and Confirmation—two sacraments whose planning and preparation programs are often the responsibility of DREs.

This chapter does not pretend to offer a comprehensive treatment of any of the five sacraments discussed. Again, my hope is that the comments I make and the reflections I offer here will encourage you to continue your study and reflection of these sacraments by consulting other, more detailed, resources.

THE SACRAMENT OF RECONCILIATION

"No one goes to Confession anymore. . . It isn't as important to Catholics as it once was . . . We don't need to go to Confession as much as we used to because the way we look at sin has changed." Comments such as these are heard in parishes throughout the country.

Some Catholics truly lament the diminishing number of long lines forming in a dimly lit church on a Saturday afternoon. Others see this phenomenon simply as a sign that private confession is a thing of the past. They might say that communal services of Reconciliation—or General Absolution—are the way the Church should celebrate this sacrament in the future.

I will forgo the risky business of predicting the Church's future confessional practice. My interest here is to discuss the practice of sacramental Reconciliation (once called Confession) as we have the opportunity to experience it now.

SOME MYTHS ABOUT THE SACRAMENT OF RECONCILIATION

First, I respond to three comments about the sacrament of Reconciliation that I often hear. I call these comments "myths," for they are based upon a faulty or incomplete understanding, not only of the sacrament of Reconciliation, but also of the sacraments in general.

First myth: "We don't need Reconciliation because our sins are forgiven through Baptism and the Eucharist."

Response: The Church does teach that venial sins are forgiven by means other than the sacrament—true contrition, works of charity, prayer, and by the grace conferred as we celebrate the Eucharist or any of the sacraments. In this sense, then, it is true that we do not "need" the sacrament of Reconciliation to forgive these venial or "ordinary" sins (see *CCC*, #1434–1439 for an extended discussion of this). Concerning mortal sins, however, Church teaching is clear:

> Individual, integral confession [the private encounter between priest and penitent in which

the penitent confesses his or her specific sins]
and absolution remain the only ordinary way for
the faithful to reconcile themselves with God
and the Church, unless physical or moral
impossibility excuses [them] from this kind of
confession. (*Rite of Penance*, #31)

Apart from extraordinary circumstances, therefore (for
example, the absence of a confessor, or our personal or
professional relationship with the only confessor available), sacramental Reconciliation is the ordinary way by
which Catholics are forgiven grave or mortal sins.

Some would counter by insisting that God does not
"need" the sacrament of Reconciliation to forgive even
mortal sins. This is certainly true. As we have discussed, it
is traditional Catholic teaching that God's grace does not
rely upon, nor is it bound to, the seven sacraments. God
does not need the sacrament—*but we do*, for the sacraments are more than the promise and efficacious sign that
God acts on our behalf. They are these, but they are
more. A sacramental celebration is a way we, as members
of Christ's Church, respond to God's action in and
through that Church.

Second myth: "You don't need to go to Reconciliation
unless you have committed a mortal sin."

Response: Not only does the Church recommend that
venial sins be confessed, but this practice makes good
sense. Many Christians lead good and holy lives and seldom, if ever, commit serious sin. But we all do things—or
we do not do things—for which the appropriate response
can only be, "I am sorry." Whenever we recognize that we
have hurt someone, when we lie or are unkind or rude,
when we turn away in the face of another's need, whenever
we recognize that we have consciously or unconsciously
"missed the mark"—in short, whenever we forget that
"just as you did it to one of the least of these who are

members of my family, you did it to me" (Matthew 25:40)—we should consider making the conscious effort to acknowledge our sin and seek the grace of God that Reconciliation offers.

Of course, the confessional is not a spiritual washing machine, and confessing our sins, as important as that is, does not mean that the hurt or pain we have caused another is automatically undone or "taken care of." But it is an important step in holding ourselves accountable for what we have done or have failed to do (see *CCC*, #1455).

As in the celebration of all the sacraments, the ideal is that the spirit, or the grace, of our confession will endure long after we have celebrated the sacrament and have returned to our homes, friends, and work. The sacrament is not a time of magical healing, but a response on our part to commit ourselves to do all that we can "to make a new future possible," to heal others through the contrition we have expressed and the grace we have received. What we have begun by confessing in church, we should continue by making amends in our public lives. We are offered the gift of Reconciliation; we must "unwrap" it.

Third myth: "It is useless to confess sins we know we will be committing again."

Response: Celebrating the sacrament does not guarantee we will never sin again. Rather, regular celebration of the sacrament assists us in committing ourselves to continue to address and be accountable even for those frequent sins for which we may be guilty. In other words, regular celebration of the sacrament guarantees that we will not let ourselves off the hook. To not go to Reconciliation because we confess the same old things over and over is throwing up our hands and surrendering to the alleged impossibility of breaking old habits, rather than remembering who we are called to be and so opening our arms and consciously surrendering once more to the grace of God.

MEANINGS OF THE SACRAMENT OF RECONCILIATION

The sacrament of Reconciliation reconciles us with God and with the Church. In other words, the sacrament helps us honor the two great commandments given by Jesus, to:

> 'love the Lord your God with all your heart,
> and with all your soul, and with all your mind,
> and with all your strength. . . . [and] love your
> neighbor as yourself.' (Mark 12:30–31)

The sacrament is not only the celebration by and through which we are reconciled with God and our Church; it also has "a revitalizing effect on the life of the Church" (*CCC*, #1469). The sacrament revitalizes the Church, because the sacrament revitalizes those who celebrate it; we can receive new life, new insights, and new aid to keep us on the right path. I mention briefly three of these insights or aids that are offered us through the sacrament.

A call to accountability: The sacrament of Reconciliation is a call to accountability. Whenever we examine our consciences, we are calling ourselves to accountability. We are "taking count" of our lives and our responsibilities. Considered in this way, an examination of conscience is not simply designed to help us answer the question: "What have I done wrong?" or "What good have I left undone?" Examining our conscience—taking account of our lives—is to remind us, as Saint Paul says in his Letter to the Romans, that we neither live nor die to ourselves but to the Lord (see 14:7), and that each of us is charged with "the good purpose of building up the neighbor" (15:2). As we discussed in Chapter 5, one way of understanding Baptism is that it is a "change of ownership and allegiance."

A return to grace: We may also consider the sacrament as a return to grace. By this I mean more than the fact that, through the celebration of the sacrament, those who have committed mortal sins are forgiven and are, therefore, returned to a state of grace. The sacrament is an opportunity for all Christians to return to the awareness and appreciation of God's grace—a grace that makes possible all we do. The Letter to the Ephesians makes this clear:

> For by grace you have been saved through faith, and this is not your own doing; it is the gift of God—not the result of works, so that no one may boast. (2:8–9)

The more we return to God's grace—the more we approach this grace as gift—the more we will adopt humility and thanksgiving as two attitudes toward life that should be characteristic of all Christians.

A making real to us the truth of God's forgiveness of our sins: The sacrament of Reconciliation makes the truth of God's forgiveness of our sins more real to us. (Recall that this is a fundamental understanding of what the sacraments do, a point stressed throughout this booklet.) The Incarnation proved once and for all that God does not deal with us only in theory. God's Son took on our flesh and lived our life so that we might learn to live his. The very thing that many find difficult in confessing their sins to a priest—that is, stating specific sins—is also one of the unique gifts the sacrament offers: the *specific* response of God's forgiveness to the *specific* situation of a *specific* penitent is expressed most clearly by the confessor's *specific* response.

Some Practical Points

• *How often should I go to Reconciliation?*

The best response I have heard to this question comes from a friend who teaches religion in an elementary grade school. She asks her students, "How often do you need to say I am sorry?"

The answers vary, and can best be answered by talking with a priest or a spiritual director. For those who have been away for a long time, it might be helpful to confess monthly—to get back into the habit. Others who are not conscious of grave sins may find the beginning of the seasons of the year a helpful pattern. Still others—those who are undergoing a particularly difficult time in their lives, for example, or those who are involved in work wherein they give but seem to receive very little—may find monthly (or even more frequent) confession to be helpful. Remember, one of the values of Reconciliation is not just that our sins are forgiven, but that this sacrament of forgiveness is a time for us to acknowledge what we receive from the Church and from God.

• *How do I prepare for the sacrament of Reconciliation?*

Ideally, preparation to celebrate the sacrament should begin a few days ahead of time. This is particularly true when we are trying to establish a habit of confessing. The initial preparation may be a matter of "setting the stage"—or, more appropriately, of setting our hearts toward that which we seek: God's pardon and peace. There are, literally, hundreds of passages in the Scriptures that can assist us in this regard. As an example, I add a brief comment to three passages that seem to me to be particularly poignant for those preparing to celebrate the sacrament.

• Isaiah 55:3: "Incline your ear, and come to me; listen, so that you may live." Let us give the Word of the Lord time to sink in and take root in our hearts. And, as any farmer can testify, patience is a necessary habit for those waiting for the seed to bear fruit.

• Luke 5:8: Peter says, "Go away from me, Lord, for I am a sinful man!" After the miraculous catch of fish, Peter actually pleads with Jesus to leave him; he feels he is not worthy to be close to one who is so great. We do well to remember the Lord's response to Peter's request; it is one of the few times in the Gospels when Jesus says "No."

• Mark 10:49, 51: "And they called the blind man [Bartimaeus], saying to him, 'Take heart; get up, he is calling you' . . . Then Jesus said to him, 'What do you want me to do for you?'" How would we respond if Jesus asked us, in the context of the sacrament, "What is it you want me to do for you?"

• *How do I examine my conscience?*

Examinations of conscience can be found in many prayer books and leaflets, as well as in virtually all Sunday or weekday missals published for the use of all Christians. We might begin with these, or by answering the question: "Who am I?" There are several answers to this question, of course: "I am a husband. I am a father. I am an office worker. I am a cradle Catholic." The many answers we might offer to the question "Who am I?" provide a basic framework for an examination of conscience. For example: "I am a husband." Therefore I ask: "What do I need to pay attention to so that I can become a better husband? Does the way I treat my wife truly reflect that I do love her? If strangers were to spend a few days in our house, would they leave knowing that I love my wife deeply?" Another example: "I am a father." Therefore I ask: "Am I giving a good example to my children? When my children listen to me and watch me, are they learning the things I want them to learn?" And yet another example: "I work in an office." Therefore I ask: "Would my co-workers know that I am a Christian by the way I work or the way I talk about others? And even if I feel that I am not paid enough, am I at least putting in an honest day's work for what I do get paid?" A final example: "I am a cradle Catholic." Therefore I ask: "Do I take my faith for granted? When was the last time I consciously, deliberately tried to learn something about my Church and what it teaches? Having been born into the Church, are there ways in which I can live more for and in the Church?"

Another kind of examination of conscience is biblically founded. As an example, we can consider three of the great stories in the first part of the Book of Genesis, and ask how we do or do not continue to contribute to the history of sin. Pope John Paul II refers to this in his Apostolic Exhortation, *Reconciliation and Penance*. For example, there is the sin of Adam and Eve: the sin of direct disobedience against God (see Genesis 3). How have we sinned in this way? How have we turned away from the gifts God has given us? Then there is the sin of Cain against his brother Abel (see Genesis 4). How have we hurt others? Do we have an attitude that suggests we think of ourselves as our brothers' and sisters' keepers? Do we try to *be* their brothers or sisters? Finally there is the sin of the tower builders of Babel (see Genesis 11). In this story we find what is perhaps one of the most frequent sins of our time: good people who do good things, but whose sin is to forget God in the doing of it all.

THE SACRAMENT OF THE ANOINTING OF THE SICK

Just as the preconciliar understanding of this sacrament reflected its name—*Extreme Unction*, the "last anointing"—so, too, is our understanding of this sacrament's significance now reflected in the "recovered" designation of the sacrament as the *Anointing of the Sick*. No longer is the sacrament reserved "until or near the moment of death," for no longer is the sacrament understood primarily as a spiritual healing alone. Referring to our discussion in Chapter 4 of the changing "attitude" of the Church toward why the sacraments are celebrated, we might say that this sacrament helps us be sick in the way Christians should be sick. The *Catechism of the Catholic Church* offers two fine paragraphs that lead us into this thought. Although some people may think that we suffer illness because we sin (for Jesus' rebuttal of this attitude, see his encounter with the blind man in John 9), the *CCC* offers us a better perspective: we may sin *because we are sick* (see #1500).

The "new" (postconciliar) understanding of this sacrament can be seen clearly, as we have already indicated, by comparing the pre- and postconciliar matter and form of the sacrament. No longer does the priest anoint the senses of the dying person, asking God to forgive whatever sins have been committed through them. Now the forehead and hands (and, as the rite allows, the physical site of the illness or pain) are anointed with the prayer that "the Lord in his love and mercy [may] help you with the grace of the Holy Spirit," and that the Lord may "save you and raise you up." The change in emphasis is significant: not an anointing and forgiveness of sins so that the dying person may be "ready for heaven" but rather, an anointing of grace so that the sick person may follow the example of the suffering Christ and so persevere as Christ persevered. This new understanding of the sacrament does not deny death; rather, it is a reminder that, even as Christians suffer through illness—even as Christians approach death—there is still "work to be done." It is the work of continuing to place our trust and hope in God.

Someone once said that the trouble with most people is that they don't face death soon enough. The stark statement belies a truth we know all too well: when we are faced with death—our own or of one whom we love—or when we are confronted with a serious illness (or the scare of it), our life often changes for the better. "You change your approach, your appreciation, to life when you've made a rendezvous with death," as a friend of mine, reflecting on her own experience, likes to say. In this sense, the Anointing of the Sick helps Christians continue the "work" of their conversion on this earth. As the *CCC* notes: "Very often illness provokes a search for God and a return to him" (#1501).

WHO CAN BE ANOINTED?

Noting that the sacrament of the Anointing of the Sick is not only for those who are at the point of death, the Second Vatican Council's *Sacrosanctum Concilium* (*SC*) said that:

> . . . as soon as anyone of the faithful begins to be in danger of death from sickness or old age, the fitting time for him to receive this sacrament has certainly already arrived. (#73)

But, something else happened by the time the Church's new *Code of Canon Law* was promulgated twenty years later. There, the phrase "in danger of death" had been modified to "in danger." This is consistent with the *CCC*'s claim, as we cited above, that illness and suffering can "provoke a search for God and a return to him (#1501)"— or it can lead to anguish and revolt against God. (Curiously, the *CCC* [#1514] quotes the *SC* and only refers to the *Code of Canon Law*, thus retaining the phrase, "in danger of death." Legislative weight here would be given the *Code*.) The important question is no longer, "How close to death is this person?" but "Is this person's illness and suffering causing 'danger,' physical danger or—more importantly, in the context of this sacrament—spiritual danger?"

Given this, the sacrament is not reserved to the dying or the grievously ill. Proper candidates for Anointing are those who are struggling, spiritually and physically, with their sickness—or with the aging process. The sacrament is for those who need help—the help of the Church, the spiritual grace and strength offered by the sacrament—in living with their deteriorating physical condition.

The Sacrament Is for "More People" than in the Past—But It Is Not for Everyone

While we must make sure that those who would benefit from celebrating this sacrament are not denied it until it is too late, we must assure also that we do not abuse the sacrament. In some parishes, communal anointings are often introduced by the priest inviting everyone to be anointed: "We are all sick and in need of healing in some way or another," is the oft-heard claim. The intention here is understandable, but the pastoral execution is shallow. We *are* all in need of healing, and for most of us the sacrament of Reconciliation is the proper sacrament to approach. Furthermore, when individual ministers expand the Church's understanding of the sacrament of Anointing of the Sick to include everyone, then the special attention given to the proper candidates and the special meaning the sacrament has for them are compromised.

"BEING SICK IN A CHRISTIAN WAY" IS A VOCATION

The sacrament of the Anointing of the Sick traditionally has been considered, along with Reconciliation, a sacrament of healing. Following the traditional division, Baptism, Confirmation, and Eucharist are the sacraments of initiation; Holy Orders and Matrimony are considered the vocation sacraments. Surely it is not difficult to see Anointing as a sacrament of healing.

But to conclude our discussion of Anointing, we may also consider this sacrament as one of vocation: a commissioning of the sick Christian to witness to those of us who enjoy good health (and are often distracted by being healthy). The message is that our ultimate and lasting strength is found only in Christ (see *CCC*, #1521).

THE "LAST SACRAMENT" IS THE EUCHARIST RECEIVED AS VIATICUM

There is a "last sacrament" for Christians, but it is the Eucharist received as *Viaticum*. *Viaticum* comes from the combining of two Latin words whose joint meaning suggests the concept of "a companion on the way." The *CCC* notes that the three sacraments of Reconciliation, Anointing of the Sick, and Viaticum, the "sacraments that complete the earthly pilgrimage," complement and complete the three sacraments that initiate one's life in the Spirit— Baptism, Confirmation, and the Eucharist (see #1525). It also speaks to the appropriateness of the Eucharist received as Viaticum as the Christian's "last sacrament" (see #1524).

THE SACRAMENT OF MATRIMONY

DREs ordinarily will not be involved professionally with the sacrament of Matrimony, but many will have a personal investment in one. I offer, then, a few comments about contemporary Church teaching and understanding of marriage, not as a civil institution, but as a sacrament—a "door to the sacred," a hidden treasure of God's grace.

OUR WORLD NEEDS A SACRAMENT OF MATRIMONY

Given the sociology of marriage today, some would argue that the Church has no place in the matrimonial business. "There are too many divorces . . . A life-time commitment is simply not possible for many people . . . Catholics should 'marry like anyone else,' and just follow the civil rules and regulations governing marriage." These and similar statements suggest that the Church's teaching on wedlock presents a needless complication at best, an unfair burden at worst, to many Christian men and women.

In the face of what seems to be an age of "quickie marriages" and even more rapid divorces, I suggest that what
today's society needs is the very witness to marriage that
the Church offers through its teaching: that a sacramental
union goes far beyond the marriage contract regulated by
society. Matrimony is a covenant, "'by which a man and a
woman establish between themselves a partnership of the
whole of life'" (*Code of Canon Law*, #1055 §1).

In my opinion, one of the most beautiful lines in the
CCC is found in the section on Matrimony. After quoting
the conciliar document *Gaudium et spes* (*The Pastoral Constitution on the Church in the Modern World*) and reminding
us that "God himself is the author of marriage" (#1603),
the *CCC* remarks:

> God who created man out of love also calls him
> to *love—the fundamental and innate vocation of
> every human being*. (#1604; emphasis added)

What an astounding series of statements! God is the
author of marriage. God writes the text and knows the
plot that, over the course of a lifetime, will develop
between *this* man and *this* woman and so continue the
work of creation. And love is a *vocation*: a way—for this
man and this woman, *the* way—in and through which they
will "unwrap the gifts" God has given each of them for the
benefit of themselves and their families.

MATRIMONY AS A CONSECRATED VOCATION

The *CCC* treats Matrimony and Holy Orders together, in
a section entitled "The Sacraments at the Service of Communion." What these two sacraments have in common, it
explains, is that Matrimony and Holy Orders:

> . . . are directed towards the salvation of others; if
> they contribute as well to personal salvation, it is
> through service to others that they do so. (#1534)

Matrimony is the special sacrament through which husband and wife contribute to each other's holiness and, in so doing, grow in holiness themselves. Matrimony is a sacrament of mutual ministry, a "partnership of ministry": husband ministers to wife, wife ministers to husband, and both—having "established between themselves a partnership of the whole of life" (*Code of Canon Law*, #1055 §1)—minister and so are instruments of grace for their children. Matrimony is a distinctive sacrament in that the ministers of the sacrament are the husband and wife (not the priest).

As with the other sacraments, the sacrament of Matrimony—the conferral of God's grace through the sacrament—does not come to an end once the liturgical celebration of Matrimony has concluded. Matrimony is a continuing sacrament, an ongoing ministering of God's grace, one spouse to the other. As the Second Vatican Council's *LG* says:

> In virtue of the sacrament of Matrimony by which they signify and share (cf. Eph. 5:32) the mystery of the unity and faithful love between Christ and the Church, Christian married couples help one another to attain holiness in their married life and in the rearing of their children. Hence by reason of their state in life and of their position they have their own gifts in the people of God (cf. 1 Cor. 7:7). (*LG*, #11)

The defining word in the phrase "Christian marriage" is *Christian*. A Christian marriage must be different than society's marriage. Premarital reflection—and, especially, postmarital reflection—must continue to address this question: "How is my marriage different? How is my marriage *Christian*? How is my marriage a 'door to the sacred' for my spouse and my children? What are the hidden treasures of God's love and grace that I can offer to the one who shares with me this 'partnership of the whole of life?'"

THE SACRAMENT OF HOLY ORDERS

Although DREs will seldom, if ever, be involved professionally with the sacrament of Holy Orders, it is necessary that they understand the similarities this sacrament has to the Church's other sacraments. They also need to understand this sacrament's uniqueness. I offer a few reflections concerning this sacrament.

As with Matrimony, Holy Orders traditionally has been considered one of the Church's "sacraments of vocation." As mentioned above, Holy Orders—as well as Matrimony—is directed primarily toward the salvation of others. This is not to say that the priest does not become holy through this sacrament but, as the *CCC* says:

> If [these sacraments of vocation, that is, Matrimony and Holy Orders] contribute as well to personal salvation, it is through service to others that they do so. (#1534)

PRIESTLY SERVICE AND PRIESTLY BEING

Asked to explain why the Church needs priests, most people offer a long list of things that a priest does: to preside at the Eucharist; to hear confessions; to baptize and bury people; to preach and teach. The answer is right; this is true. But it's incomplete. Just as important as what the priest does is who the priest is—and who he represents. When a priest acts, what he does is of no greater importance than in whose name he acts. This is part of what the Second Vatican Council's *Lumen Gentium* ([*LG*] *The Dogmatic Constitution on the Church*) meant when it explained that the ministerial priesthood differs from the priesthood of all the faithful not just in degree, but also in essence

(#10). As the Second Vatican Council's *Presbyterorum ordinis* (*Decree on the Ministry and Life of Priests*) expresses it, "Priests as ministers of the sacred mysteries, especially in the sacrifice of the Mass, act in a special way in the person of Christ who gave himself as a victim to sanctify men" (#13). This is what is meant by the expression that the priest acts *in persona Christi Capitis*: when the priest acts, he acts "in the person of Christ the Head" of the Church.

The Priest as Bridge-Builder

Another essential difference between the ministerial priesthood and the priesthood of all the faithful concerns in whose name the priest fulfills his ministry. The priest acts not only in the name and person of Christ, but also in the name of the community to whom he ministers. The priest is a representation, an effective symbol of Christ: he represents Christ to the community by what he does and through his presence. But the priest also "presents" the community to Christ, and is therefore a representation of his people: their wants, sufferings, needs, and desires. To refer to the classic Latin word, the priest is a *pontifex*, a "bridge-builder" between God and humankind:

> The ministerial priest, by the sacred power that he has, forms and rules the priestly people; in the person of Christ he effects the eucharistic sacrifice and offers it to God in the name of all the people. (*LG*, #10)

SACRAMENTAL CHARACTER AND SACRAMENTAL GRACE

Sacraments confer a religious reality (grace) and an ecclesial reality (character, in the case of Baptism, Confirmation, and Holy Orders). The grace conferred through sacramental ordination is expressed well in the essential formula of the sacrament (see Table One in Appendix I). The sacramental character emphasizes the nature of this grace, as well as again stressing the priest's acting in the name of the Eternal High Priest (see *CCC*, #1581).

THE SACRAMENT OF CONFIRMATION

It may seem ironic that the last individual sacrament discussed in this chapter is a sacrament of initiation. But the irony reflects the actual dilemma the sacrament of Confirmation faces in many parishes and dioceses today.

As we discussed in Chapter 4, the history of Confirmation is a particularly tortuous one. The field is divided into two primary camps: those who consider Confirmation a sacrament of initiation, and therefore hold that it should be conferred either at Baptism or together with one's First Communion; and those who consider it a sacrament of maturity, and therefore believe that the later the sacrament is administered, the better. Adding to the confusion surrounding Confirmation today is the fact that there is no clear indication of how this sacrament will evolve in the immediate future. In 1994, the Holy See accepted the request from the bishops of the United States that Confirmation be administered, at the decision of the individual bishop, anywhere between the ages of seven and eighteen. The request originally was for a five-year trial period, but at their 1998 meeting, the American bishops requested a three-year extension.

There is no shortage of ideas about what to do with Confirmation, and readers are encouraged to consult the three books listed in the Bibliography (see Turner and Wilde). What I will offer in our discussion here reflects, hopefully, both the situation DREs will find themselves in with regard to Confirmation, and their actual ability to influence its practice. The influence is little; the situation, frankly, is to know what the practice is in one's parish and to attempt to promote the most credible understanding of that practice that our theological reflection can allow.

CONFIRMATION IS AN INITIATION AND A COMPLETION

Baptism, Confirmation, and the Eucharist are considered the three sacraments of Christian initiation. Indeed, much of contemporary theology tries to explain how these sacraments are related one to the other, and why all three are necessary for full membership in the Church. The first two paragraphs in the Introduction to the *Rite of Confirmation* explain the significance of the sacrament and its special gifts:

> Those who have been baptized continue on the path of Christian initiation through the sacrament of confirmation. In this sacrament they receive the Holy Spirit, who was sent upon the apostles by the Lord on Pentecost. (#1)

> This giving of the Holy Spirit conforms believers more perfectly to Christ and strengthens them so that they may bear witness to Christ for the building up of his body in faith and love. They are so marked with the character or seal of the Lord that the sacrament of confirmation cannot be repeated. (#2)

It is easier to understand how Christian initiation "remains incomplete" without the reception of the Eucharist, than it does without the benefit of Confirmation. The *CCC* insists that "Confirmation is necessary for the completion of baptismal grace" (#1285), but its attempt to add clarification seems to lend some complexity as well:

> Although Confirmation is sometimes called the 'sacrament of Christian maturity,' we must not confuse adult faith with the adult age of natural growth, nor forget that the baptismal grace is a grace of free, unmerited election and does not need 'ratification' to become effective. (#1308)

The *CCC* then quotes Saint Thomas Aquinas, who stated that "age of body does not determine age of soul," and that "many children, through the strength of the Holy Spirit they have received, have bravely fought for Christ even to the shedding of their blood" (*Summa Theologica* III, 72, 8, *ad* 2). These statements seem to reinforce the idea that Confirmation is a sacrament of *Christian*, if not human, maturity. While the *CCC* rightly stresses that baptismal (and all) grace is "free and unmerited," its description of baptismal grace as needing "completion" but not "ratification" is a distinction that is unlikely to offer much help to our parishioners.

WHAT *ARE* THE EFFECTS OF CONFIRMATION?

As indicated in our Table One, the form—the core words—of the sacrament of Confirmation is expressed by the simple statement, "Be sealed with the gift of the Holy Spirit." The bishop's homily or instruction to those about to be confirmed offers some additional, helpful commentary on the meaning of this sacrament:

> The gift of the Holy Spirit which you are to receive will be a spiritual sign and seal to make you more like Christ and more perfect members of his Church. . . . You have already been baptized into Christ and now you will receive the power of his Spirit and the sign of the cross on your forehead. You must be witnesses before all the world to his suffering, death, and resurrection; your way of life should at all times reflect the goodness of Christ. . . . Be active members of the Church, alive in Jesus Christ. Under the guidance of the Holy Spirit give your lives completely in the service of all, as did Christ, who came not to be served but to serve. (*Rite of Confirmation*, #22)

The bishop's instruction reflects what we have already discussed: that sacraments confer an "ecclesial reality" as well as a spiritual one (grace). In the case of Confirmation, as in the case with Baptism and Holy Orders, this sacrament confers an indelible mark upon the soul—the sacramental character—that "perfects the common priesthood of the faithful, received in Baptism" (*CCC*, #1305), so that those confirmed receive the grace and the power to witness their faith in Christ to the world and in the name of the Church.

CONFIRMATION IN THE PARISH—PRACTICALLY SPEAKING

The *CCC* offers two helpful themes, or "markers," in which preparation for Confirmation should be grounded: first, that preparation should lead the candidate "to be more capable of assuming the apostolic responsibilities of Christian life"; second, that "catechesis for Confirmation should strive to awaken a sense of belonging to the Church of Jesus Christ, the universal Church as well as the parish community" (#1309). Let us consider each of these two markers—and a third one as well.

Assuming the apostolic responsibilities of Christian life: Much of this booklet has emphasized that the sacraments are not rituals confined to a celebration in church, but rather liturgical celebrations that provide us with the spiritual resources and encouragement to continue to live out the meaning of the sacrament in the world. Certainly, the *CCC*'s first suggested marker for catechesis about Confirmation confirms this concept.

What are the "apostolic responsibilities of Christian life"? The *CCC*'s article nine ("I believe in the Holy Catholic Church") of Part One ("The Profession of Faith") offers a brief explanation of what we mean by "the apostolate" (see # 863–865). Paragraph #863 reminds us that "all members of the Church share in [the Church's mission], though in various ways." The next paragraph states that, while "the apostolate assumes the most varied forms," it is "charity, drawn from the Eucharist above all, [that] is always 'as it were, the soul of the whole apostolate'" (#864).

A subsequent section within the same article is even more specific. An excellent section on "The Lay Faithful" (see #897–913) reminds us that the laity are "to seek the kingdom of God by engaging in temporal affairs and directing them according to God's will" (*LG*, #31). This directing of temporal affairs according to God's will is both the *right* and the *duty* of those who have been confirmed (see *CCC*, #900).

I suggest that accompanying sections in the *CCC* provide more than adequate material upon which DREs may reflect, and so prepare candidates of whatever age for "unwrapping the gift" that Confirmation bestows upon them.

A sense of belonging to the Church of Jesus Christ, the universal Church: Commenting upon the practice of the Eastern Churches (which always confirm at the time of Baptism), the *CCC* explains:

> The practice of the Eastern Churches gives greater emphasis to the unity of Christian initiation. That of the Latin Church more clearly expresses the communion of the new Christian with the bishop as guarantor and servant of the unity, catholicity and apostolicity of his Church, and hence the connection with the apostolic origins of Christ's Church. (#1292)

The second "catechetical marker" that the *CCC* offers us is found in the very reasons why, in the tradition of our Western Church, Confirmation ordinarily is reserved to the bishop. Administered by the bishop of one's diocese,

Confirmation will encourage candidates to look beyond their own communities and so understand that they belong not to one parish, no matter how large or small, urban or rural, but to the entire Body of Christ on Earth. Catechesis for Confirmation, therefore, should in some way speak of the importance of the ministry of the bishop, as well as what the Church teaches about apostolic succession, unity, and catholicity. (Explanations and commentaries on these teachings are found in Part One of the *CCC*.) Those preparing for Confirmation should know that they belong to a Church that has a history in the world, a Church that has, more than once, changed the course of the world's history.

Completion of Baptism; an increase and deepening of baptismal grace: As noted above, the *CCC* speaks often of Confirmation as "perfecting" or "completing" the grace first received at Baptism. Catechesis for Baptism, then, should include the continuation of the postbaptismal catechesis that, ideally, lasts throughout one's Christian life. Although many of the people DREs work with will have no memory of their Baptism, this does not mean that these people cannot be led to understand the significance and meaning of what was "done to them." In line with this, the short essay on the concept of "Infant Baptism as our Adoption by God" in Appendix II provides some initial reflections.

Finally, other essential elements in catechesis for Confirmation have been referred to throughout this booklet: that the sacraments are the "verbs" of Christian life; that the sacraments should define the way we act; that all Christians share in the priesthood of Christ; and that "vocation" is not a concept to be applied only to priests and religious leaders.

We have reflected upon two sacraments, Baptism and Eucharist, in some detail, and have reviewed the essential teachings of the Church concerning the sacraments of Reconciliation, Anointing of the Sick, Matrimony, Holy Orders, and Confirmation. The following "Conclusion" highlights the major themes of our discussion.

CHAPTER SUMMARY

1. The sacrament of Reconciliation is the only ordinary way for the faithful to reconcile themselves with God and the Church. However, this sacrament, which makes God's forgiveness and mercy more real to us, ideally does not conclude when we leave the confessional. As with all the sacraments, the gift of the sacrament carries with it the responsibility of our "unwrapping that gift." We are reconciled with God so that we may be reconciled with others. (Refer to our discussion of the parable of the unworthy servant in Chapter 3.)

2. The sacrament of the Anointing of the Sick helps Christians confront their illnesses, suffering, or death as Christians should: with trust and hope in the Lord's help and his grace. The special vocation of the sick and suffering is to witness their belief that God is the ultimate source of strength and grace of us all.

3. The sacrament of Matrimony, a covenant that involves "a partnership of the whole of life" (*Code of Canon Law*, #1055 §1), is a partnership of love and of ministry. Through their marriage, husbands and wives receive a particular mission in the Church: a mission for the good of the Church, as well as for their own growth in holiness.

4. The ministerial priesthood differs from the priesthood of all the faithful, not only in degree, but also in essence. The priest represents Christ to his community,

and acts in his name. Similarly, the priest prays in the name of the whole Church to our Father in heaven.

5. The pastoral practice of Confirmation may vary from diocese to diocese, but there are several common elements that should be included in preparing candidates, of whatever age, for this sacrament. These include assisting candidates to understand and assume their responsibilities in sharing in the apostolic work of the Church, and instilling in them a sense that our Church is "one, holy, Catholic, and apostolic." Preparation for Confirmation also provides an ideal occasion for candidates to reflect more upon—and so "thoroughly unwrap"—the grace of their Baptism.

FOR REFLECTION

1. How can the sacrament of Reconciliation contribute to our spiritual life, even though (or perhaps especially when) we are not guilty of grave or serious sins? How can we prepare to celebrate this sacrament so that it will, indeed, make such a contribution?

2. What does it mean to say that, in addition to being considered a sacrament of healing, the sacrament of the Anointing of the Sick may also be understood as a vocational sacrament? How can we help those who are ill understand that they can minister to us?

3. How can husbands and wives be "instruments of grace" to each other? In relation to our previous statement, that Christ is the "first sacrament" of God the Father, how might husbands and wives be the "first sacrament of Christ" to each other and to their families?

4. What does it mean to say that the priest is a "bridge-

builder" between God and humankind?

5. How can eight-year-old children bear witness to their faith? How can adolescents be expected to do this? How can we encourage and assist both young children and adolescents to see Confirmation as a "deepening and completion of their baptismal grace"? How can we give candidates for Confirmation a sense of the wider Catholic Church that exists outside of their own parish or diocese?

Conclusion

This "Conclusion" is less an attempt to summarize the entire work, and more an effort to review what I consider to be the more important insights or perspectives emerging from our discussion of the sacraments.

1. The liturgy is the most important work *of* the Church and *for* the Church. It is work certainly in our effort to come together as Church. It is work even more in that we must allow the liturgy to continue to work in our lives in the world.

2. Sacraments are not abstract Catholic concepts. Rather, they are earthy symbols that speak to our imaginations as much as they do to our minds. Through the "visible words" that the sacraments are, we touch—and we are touched by—Christ, the fundamental sacrament of God's love for us.

3. Grace is a gift, freely given by God, given at God's initiative. We can receive grace only as we receive a gift, for grace is not something we earn or deserve. This gift, however, does not come cheap and it does come with "strings attached": for the gift of grace is accompanied by the responsibility of responding to that grace.

4. Each of the sacraments has a complex (and sometimes tortuous) history. The basic instinct behind each of the

140

seven sacraments, however, can be seen in the earliest practices of the Church, as they are grounded firmly in the person of Jesus Christ.

5. Especially during the age of the Scholastic theologians (eleventh through the fourteenth centuries), scholars were intent on discovering exactly where in the Scriptures Christ instituted each of the seven sacraments. Affirming the teaching of the Church that Christ did institute each of the sacraments, our approach today can be quite different. It is less important for us to "find out" when Christ instituted each of the sacraments, and more important that we remember that Christ came to *be the* sacrament of God's love for humankind. Understanding what this means—and learning what our response to this mission of Christ should be—is, for Christians, the work of a lifetime—the work we call *conversion*.

I offer as a list of reflections some descriptions of what we mean by sacraments and what the sacraments "do." Each of these descriptions should invite further reflection upon the traditional definition of a sacrament, that it is "a visible sign instituted by Christ to give grace."

1. The sacraments don't simply tell us that something is true; they try to make the truth more real to us.

2. Our celebration of the sacraments of the Church continues to reveal God's love for humankind through the person and work of Jesus Christ.

3. The sacraments are the essential markers, key orientations, and spiritual resources that show Christians how—and enable them—to respond to the love of God.

4. The sacraments are not "sacred parentheses" in the lives of individual Christians or of the Church. The sacra-

ments are the "verbs" of Christian life, prayer, and work.

5. When the Church celebrates the sacraments, she is again defining herself. The sacraments are the Church in action in the lives of her members for their benefit and the benefit of all the world.

To conclude where we began: "Actions speak louder than words." The sacraments are visible words of Christ and of the Church. As such, their ritual prayers must not be mutely recited, nor should their symbols and liturgical actions be seen as empty gestures. The visible words of the sacraments are words we must allow to speak to us: to speak to us loudly and clearly, to speak to us in a way that both guides us in our Christian way of life and challenges us to be true to that way of life. The sacraments may consist of visible words that we hear, see, and experience while we are in church. But we must incorporate these visible words into our lives. Only then will the sacraments have a life outside the Church. Only then will the Church have a life outside of her places of formal worship. And then—only then—will the sacraments continue to give the Church the life she needs so that she may truly be the light of the world.

Appendix 1

TABLE ONE

THE MATTER AND FORM—THE "VISIBLE WORDS"—OF THE SACRAMENTS

Sacrament	Matter	Form
Baptism	The action with water (pouring or immersion)	I baptize you in the name of the Father, and of the Son, and of the Holy Spirit.
Confirmation	The anointing of the forehead with chrism	Be sealed with the gift of the Holy Spirit.
Eucharist	Bread and wine	This is my body . . . This is my blood.
Reconciliation	The "confession" of the penitent: the acknowledgment of and sorrow for one's sinfulness, and the intention of avoiding sin in the future.	God, the Father of mercies, through the death and resurrection of his Son has reconciled the world to himself and sent the Holy Spirit among us for the forgiveness of sins; through the ministry of the Church may God give you pardon and peace, and I absolve you from your sins in the name of the Father, and of the Son, † and of the Holy Spirit. (Amen.)
Anointing of the Sick	The anointing of the forehead and hands of the sick with the oil	Through this holy anointing may the Lord in his love and mercy help you with the grace of the Holy Spirit. (Amen.) May the Lord who frees you from sin save you and raise you up. (Amen.)
Matrimony	The mutual exchange of vows between man and woman, given with full consent and freedom	
Holy Orders	The bishop imposing his hands over the candidate	Almighty Father, grant to this servant of yours the dignity of the priesthood. Renew within him the Spirit of holiness. As a co-worker with the order of bishops may he be faithful to the ministry that he receives from you, Lord God, and be to others a model of right conduct.

TABLE TWO

IMAGES OF BAPTISM IN THE SCRIPTURES, THE LITURGICAL TEXTS, AND THE *CCC*

Baptism is . . .	Scripture reference	RCIA text	RBC text	*CCC* text
a change of *Ownership*: we are claimed by God as God's own; we become God's property, God's instruments	2 Cor 1:21–22 Eph 1:13–14	par. 54–55	par. 41	par. 1269 1270
a change of *Allegiance*: we live no longer for ourselves but for him; we owe allegiance to the Spirit	Rom 6:15–18 Rom 8:12–13	90–94 138–184	3, 39, 56, 64	1269 1270
stripping off the old man and putting on the new man who is Christ	Col 3:9–11 Gal 3:27–29	229	63	1227 1243 1265
birth to new life	Jn 3:5 Titus 3:5–7	Passim	54	1215
enlightenment	Heb 10:32 1 Pet 2:9	230	64	1216 1243
making a person a sharer in Christ, the anointed king and priest	2 Cor 1:21 1 Pet 2:9	98–103 228 231–236	49–52 62	1241 1268
adoption as God's child	Rom 8:14–17, 23 Gal 4:4–5 Eph 1:3	General Introduction to Christian Initiation, pars. 1,2,5		1265

TABLE THREE
THE STAGES AND STEPS OF THE RCIA

Stage	Purpose	Features / Liturgies	Stage analogous to	Step to next stage
PRE-CATECHUMENATE Inquirers, Sympathizers	Right intention → Faith	Conversations Prayers Blessings Exorcisms [?]	~ Initial meetings with vocation director ~ Initial meetings between possible future spouses	**RITE OF ACCEPTANCE INTO THE ORDER OF CATECHUMENS**
CATECHUMENATE Catechumens Formal relationship w/ Church established	Faith → Conversion	**CATECHESIS** • Church teachings • Liturgy & prayer • Apostolic works **RITES** • Liturgies of Word • Minor exorcisms • Blessings • Anointings	~ Seminary ~ Dating period	**RITE OF ELECTION AND ENROLLMENT**
PURIFICATION & ENLIGHTENMENT Elect Competentes Illuminandi	Faith → Purification & enlightenment	**SCRUTINIES** • III Lent—John 4 • IV Lent—John 9 • V Lent—John 11 **PRESENTATIONS** • Creed • Lord's Prayer	~ "Last year in seminary" ~ Engagement / pre-cana meetings	**SACRAMENTS OF CHRISTIAN INITIATION** • Baptism • Confirmation • Eucharist
MYSTAGOGY Neophytes	Support Faith → Faith → Action	Masses for neophytes	~ Support group, continuing education	

Appendix II: Infant Baptism as Our Adoption by God

As I indicated in Chapter 4, the model of Baptism as participation in the death and resurrection of the Lord may not be the most effective or appropriate model to invoke when approaching the sacrament of infant Baptism. To the extent this is true, it is true not because of the inadequacy of rite or model, but because of the mystery of Baptism itself: a mystery that cannot be captured or expressed completely by any one theological model or ritual celebration.

The opening paragraphs of the General Introduction that introduces the Church's rites of initiation (RCIA) describe the effects of Baptism in several ways. Through Baptism "we are freed from the power of darkness and joined to Christ's death, burial, and resurrection (#1)"; this first sacrament "incorporates us into Christ and forms us into God's people (#2)" for Baptism is "the door to life and to the kingdom of God (#3)" through which we are "incorporated into the Church and are built up together in the Spirit into a house where God lives (#4)".

The power of our Baptism is perhaps best described in the words of Saint Paul. Introducing the triumphant hymn that concludes Chapter 8 of his Letter to the Romans, Paul asks: "If God is for us, who is against us?" (v. 31).

And such is his confidence in God's saving action that, after cataloging the powers that will not prevail over the believer, Paul concludes that "[nothing] will be able to separate us from the love of God in Christ Jesus our Lord" (v. 39).

But what is it, exactly, that God has done? What is the grace offered to those baptized into Christ Jesus? And how does one express the consequences of this grace in the lives of "God's beloved . . . who are called to be saints" (Romans 1:7)?

To describe the effects of God's love in Christ Jesus and the new relationship God establishes with the believer through that love, Paul requisitions the idea of adoption (see Romans 8). The word occurs only five times in the New Testament, but these scant instances belie its significance. As one scholar said many years ago, a "more vivid way of describing [the Christian's] new status in Christ could hardly be conceived."

The mention of adoption today sometimes invites pity and chagrin (and, occasionally, feeble attempts at humor). But for Paul, adoption is a word of wonder, and the Christian's adoption by God is true reason to be grateful. For adoption speaks of God's boundless grace, of the conquest of freedom over slavery, of promised inheritance, and of confident expectation. Through adoption—because of adoption—the Christian receives the gift embracing and completing all gifts given to those baptized in Christ Jesus: the gift of the Spirit, through whom God may be addressed as *Abba*, Father.

> For all who are led by the Spirit of God are children of God. For you did not receive a spirit of slavery to fall back into fear, but you have received a spirit of adoption. When we cry, 'Abba! Father!' it is that very Spirit bearing witness with our spirit that we are children of God,

and if children, then heirs, heirs of God and
joint heirs with Christ—if, in fact, we suffer
with him so that we may also be glorified with
him. (Romans 8:14–17)

I suggest there are several advantages in approaching
infant Baptism through such a "theology of adoption."
Not the least of these is that adoption, as we know and
practice it today, ordinarily deals with infants or young
children (the very age group with which infant Baptism is
concerned), and that for many parents and children the
concept relates more directly and immediately to their
lived human experience than to other theological models
or motifs.

That adoption is a human act and experience with
which many today are familiar neither alters nor replaces
the theological significance of the Christian's adoption by
God; rather, it reinforces and clarifies it. I would like to
indicate here several similarities between the human experience of adoption and Paul's exposition of the Christian's adoption by God. The following points outline what
I consider to be relatively common characteristics of the
human experience of adoption, followed by accompanying
parenthetical remarks that reflect a theological orientation.

1. Adoption, the act by which one is made the child of
   another, is an act of extraordinary initiative and love.
   (God chooses us before we choose God, and God's
   adopting us points to the utter benevolence of the gift
   of grace. "Christians are made, not born," and it is
   through adoption that we are made God's sons and
   daughters and are given a status among others and a
   relationship with God to which we have no natural right
   or claim.)

2. Adoption delivers a child *from* an unfortunate or tragic
   situation and *into* an advantageous or favorable situation.

(Adoption delivers Christians from enslavement to the law of sin and death, and effects for them the freedom to walk according to the Spirit. Adoption delivers us *from* the darkness of original sin and *into* the graced environment of Christ and Church.)

3. Adopted children are identified and affiliated with—incorporated into—their new family. (As the General Introduction to the *Rite of Christian Initiation* [*RCIA*] remind us, "Baptism incorporates us into Christ and forms us into God's people. This first sacrament . . . brings us to the dignity of adopted children, . . . Hence we are called and are indeed the children of God [#2]".)

4. The objective fact and act of adoption is ordinarily irrevocable, but the adopted child's freedom of will remains intact. (Baptized Christians are marked forever as children of God. This extraordinary gift encourages, but does not demand or force, an appropriate, *graceful* response.)

5. While adopted children may always have known the fact of their adoption, they grow only gradually into the understanding and appreciation of what their adoption has meant—and continues to mean—to them. (This growth in understanding and appreciation leads hopefully to commitment—and is what we mean by "conversion.") The disparity and tension between the gift offered now and the future responsibilities entailed by that gift are reflected in Romans 8: Christians are adopted by God, yet they still await the full benefits of their adoption, the redemption of their bodies (see v. 23). Furthermore, the tension between *gift now* and *responsibilities forthcoming* is central to the Church's own understanding of infant Baptism. The *RBC*, for example, states:

> To fulfill the true meaning of the sacrament,
> children must later be formed in the faith in
> which they have been baptized. The foundation
> of this formation will be the sacrament itself
> that they have already received. Christian for-
> mation, which is their due, seeks to lead them
> gradually to learn God's plan in Christ, so that
> they may ultimately accept for themselves the
> faith in which they have been baptized. (#3)

The aspects of Baptism that a theology of adoption addresses include: the action of God and the Christian community in the initiating and effecting of the Baptism; the immediate and enduring effects of the sacrament; the desired fulfillment of the meaning of the sacrament; and the freedom and responsibility of those baptized to realize the full benefits of their Baptism. Approaching Baptism through the lens of adoption—an act that is deliberate and extraordinary—the sacrament offers strong support to our preaching that infant Baptism is not an automatic decision, a "Catholic habit" but is, rather, a deliberate choice made by parents to adopt the child of their flesh into the body of their faith.

Glossary

The glossary provides a convenient reference for, and additional information about, some of the more technical theological terms used in this booklet. Because of their mention in the text and their importance to our study, brief comments about several theologians of our Catholic tradition also are included.

Aquinas, Thomas (1225–1274): Thomas Aquinas was the most influential of the Scholastic theologians, whose writings—particularly the *Summa Theologica*—have influenced our approach to and understanding of the sacraments for well over seven centuries. The "Third Part" of the *Summa*, which deals with the sacraments, is a remarkable synthesis of the sacramental economy. Aquinas built on the work of theologians preceding him; similarly, his theological successors, as well as several important councils of our Church (Lyons, 1274; Florence, 1439; Trent, 1545–1563), relied heavily upon his exposition of sacramental theology.

Augustine (354–430): Augustine, bishop of Hippo in Africa, was one of the great theologians of the early Church. He is associated with the development of a number of concepts and Church teachings, including those concerning original sin, sacramental character, and *ex opere operato/operantis*. Augustine was also instrumental in promoting the necessity of infant Baptism, and his writings on sexuality and Christian marriage continue to be echoed in Church teaching and thought.

Character: Character has traditionally been understood as the invisible and indelible seal placed on the soul by the sacraments of Baptism, Confirmation, and Holy Orders. While the grace of these sacraments could be forfeited through sin, the seal or character remained always: thus, once validly administered, these three sacraments cannot be repeated. For example, a Lutheran joining the Catholic Church is not "re-baptized" as a Catholic, for our Church recognizes Lutheran Baptism as valid. The individual in this case would be received into the Church by his or her profession of faith (and possibly, through the sacrament of Confirmation). Aquinas understood the sacramental character as a specific power received through the three sacraments: Baptism conferred the (passive) power of being able to receive the other sacraments, while Confirmation and Holy Orders conferred the (active) powers, respectively, of witnessing to the faith and of administering the sacraments to the people. Some theologians today would consider the sacramental character—the indelible seal—also as an expression of God's faithfulness to his people (see our discussion of the parable of the prodigal son in Chapter 3).

Council of Trent: The Council took place between the years 1545 and 1563, although in that eighteen-year period it actually was in session for only about six years. Responding to the challenges and attacks of the Protestant reformers, the Council tried to clarify Catholic teaching and reform ecclesial practice and behavior. The Council of Trent was primarily a defensive Council by nature: it sought to defend the Catholic faith and specify exactly what it was that the Catholic Church taught, rather than offer an extended commentary or reflection upon it as did, for example, the Second Vatican Council. The Council of Trent ushered in a four-century period of relative uniformity and stabilization in Catholic practice and thought.

Important documents emerging from the work or directives of the Council include the *Catechism* (1566), the *Bre-
viary* (1568), the *Pius V* or *Tridentine Missal* (1570), and the
Ritual, the collection of the sacramental rites (1614). Each
of these four books has been revised thoroughly in the
three decades following the Second Vatican Council, the
most recent being the *Catechism of the Catholic Church*
(English translation, 1994).

Effectiveness: In technical terminology, effectiveness
refers to the "automatic" effect of a validly celebrated
sacrament, that is, the conferral of grace *ex opere operato*.
Effectiveness refers to the action of Christ through his
Church in the celebration of the sacraments, not to the
individual's response to that offer of grace.

Ex opere operato (opus operatum): The Latin phrase
means "from the work worked." It refers to the teaching
that, if the correct matter and form are used, if the minister intends to do what the Church does in the celebration
of this sacrament, and if the recipient places no barrier or
obstacle, then the sacrament confers grace because the primary minister of the sacrament is Christ. Put another way,
because the primary minister of the sacrament is Christ,
the lack of worthiness on the part of the minister or a less-
than-perfect approach to the sacrament by the recipient
does not hinder the grace the sacrament offers. *Ex opere
operato* is the conferral of the gift of grace. As with the
concept of effectiveness, it refers to the action of Christ
through his Church in the celebration of the sacraments,
not to the individual's response to that offer of grace.

Ex opere operantis (opus operantis): The Latin phrase
means "by the work of the worker." This is the other side
of *ex opere operato*. It refers to an individual's response to
the sacrament's conferral, or offering, of grace: that is,
does the recipient make use of the grace offered through
the sacrament so that it truly becomes fruitful in his or her

life? *Ex opere operato* (above) is the offering of the gift of grace; *ex opere operantis* is the individual's "unwrapping that gift" and so putting it to the use to which it was intended.

Form: The form of a sacrament is the formula—the essential words of prayer—during the sacramental celebration that define or give form to the symbols or gestures that are used.

Fruitfulness: In technical terminology, fruitfulness refers to the effect the sacrament has in the lives of those who celebrate it. Fruitfulness refers to the individual's response to that offer of grace. A validly celebrated sacrament is *effective* in that it confers (offers) grace; whether the sacrament is *fruitful* depends upon the *ex opere operantis*—whether and to what extent the individual unwraps the gift of grace offered and puts it to use.

Grace: Grace is our participation in the divine life offered us as a gift through God's benevolence. Grace speaks of our relationship with God more than it does as a "thing" we receive from God. Traditional sacramental teaching is that the sacraments confer grace; they communicate God's presence to us. Grace is the result of God's self-communication, and grace is the measure of the relationship we have with God. Technically, grace can be broken down into several categories: the grace of justification (Baptism), for example, or sacramental grace, or actual grace.

Liciety / licitness: This notion refers to whether the rubrics (rules and directives) governing the celebration of the sacrament were followed. Liciety is important to the integral celebration of the sacraments, but it is not as important as the notion of validity. An example of an illicit (although still valid) celebration of infant Baptism would be one in which the priest, for no compelling reason, decided to omit the pre- and postbaptismal anointings. The sacrament would be valid because the essential matter and form were used (action with water, Trinitarian formula), but it would be considered illicit because the approved rite was not followed entirely.

Lombard, Peter (d. 1160): Lombard was the first influential person who gave convincing grounds for believing that there were seven sacraments. His *Sentences*, a book collecting the opinions of various theologians, influenced, among others, Thomas Aquinas.

Matter: The matter of a sacrament is the essential symbol or gesture that, along with the form, expresses the core sacramental action. In two sacraments—Reconciliation and Matrimony—the matter is not a visible, external symbol or gesture, but is the interior disposition of those celebrating the sacrament.

Tertullian (ca. 165–ca. 225): A particularly interesting figure in the early Church, Tertullian was raised as a pagan, converted to Catholicism at the age of twenty-two, and, about nine years later, became a devoted member of the Montanist sect. This was an apocalyptic movement that maintained a strict separation from, and condemnation of, the Catholic Church. Particularly interesting in this regard are the two treatises he wrote on the Church's theology and practice of Reconciliation: the Catholic Tertullian's *On Penitence*, written around the year 204, is rebutted in several key points by the Montanist Tertullian's *On Modesty*. Tertullian's contributions to our Catholic tradition include his *On Baptism*, the earliest surviving monograph on any of the sacraments, and his *On the Prayer*, the earliest surviving treatise we have on the "Our Father." Tertullian was the first Latin writer to apply the word *Mother* to the Church.

Validity: This notion refers to whether the Church would recognize this sacrament as "one of her own." There are three requirements for a sacrament to be considered valid: the proper matter and form; the minister's intention to do what the Church does in the celebration of this sacrament; and the recipient's lack of placing an obstacle to receiving the sacrament. An example of an invalid sacrament of infant Baptism would be if wine were poured over the baby's head instead of water, or if the priest baptized the infant in the name of "the Creator, the Redeemer, and the Sanctifier," rather than baptizing the child "in the name of the Father, the Son, and Holy Spirit." If this were the case, the child would not have to be "re-baptized," strictly speaking, but would have to be baptized "for the first time" (since the "first," and invalid, Baptism is not considered a true sacrament). Central to this notion is that the sacraments are actions of the Church, not of an individual minister, and so the words that are used are those that the Church has set forth as "her" words.

Bibliography

Béguerie, Philippe and Claude Duchesneau. *How to Understand the Sacraments*. New York: Crossroad, 1991.

> Part of the "How To" series, translated from the French. This and its companion volume (*How to Understand the Liturgy*, listed below) are virtually small encyclopedias of sacramental and liturgical theology. Numerous "sidebars" explore specific topics in greater depth.

Bernardin, Joseph. *Guide for the Assembly*. Chicago: Liturgy Training Publications, 1997.

> A reissuing of *Our Communion, Our Peace, Our Promise*, the late Cardinal Bernardin's 1984 pastoral letter on the Liturgy. The publishers have added a lengthy section entitled "Bringing This Home to the Parish," which offers questions for reflection and discussion for individuals or groups interested in exploring a vision of parish Sunday liturgy rooted in the work of the Second Vatican Council.

Catechism of the Catholic Church. Washington, DC: United States Catholic Conference, 1994.

> Since its publication in English in 1994, the *Catechism* has become a rich resource for scholars and religious educators alike. Drawing on the wide spectrum of the Church's documentary tradition, the *Catechism*'s 2,865 paragraphs are divided into four sections (or "pillars") that summarize Catholic beliefs, Catholic celebrations, the Christian life, and Christian prayer. Includes "In Brief" summary sections, a subject index, and a citation index.

Champlin, Joseph M. *With Hearts Light as Feathers: The First Reconciliation of Children*. New York: Crossroad, 1995.

> Fr. Champlin describes his four-year experience developing a program for children who will receive the sacrament of Reconciliation before their First Communion. His insights will be helpful to teachers and parents alike.

Emminghaus, Johannes H. *The Eucharist: Essence, Form, Celebration*. Collegeville, MN: Liturgical Press, 1997. (Rev. ed.)

> The most "technical" of the books presented here, Emminghaus' work is still a most readable study of the history of our eucharistic prac-

tice and of the structural elements that comprise our celebration of the Eucharist today.

John Paul II. *Reconciliation and Penance (Reconciliatio et Paenitentia)*. 1983 Post-Synodal Apostolic Exhortation. Boston: Pauline Books and Media, 1984.

Pope John Paul's exhortation of nearly two decades ago remains an excellent essay on the mysteries of grace and sin, and of the important work of Reconciliation entrusted to all Christians.

Johnson, Lawrence J. *The Mystery of Faith: A Study of the Structural Elements of the Order of the Mass*. Federation of Diocesan Liturgical Commissions, 1981. Rev. ed. 1984.

This easy-to-use workbook allows for a systematic study of the structural elements of the Mass. The historical development of each element is discussed briefly, and the relevant documentation is provided. Brief reflections and suggestions for further discussion conclude each of the fifty-nine, usually one-to-three-page, sections.

Lebon, Jean. *How to Understand the Liturgy*. New York: Crossroad, 1988.

A worthy companion volume to *How to Understand the Sacraments*, listed above.

Mahoney, Roger. *Gather Faithfully Together: Guide for Sunday Mass*. Chicago: Liturgy Training Publications, 1997.

A pastoral letter by the cardinal of Los Angeles, in which he sets forth his vision of parish liturgy in the year 2000—and what it will take to get there. Part one is addressed to all the Catholics in his archdiocese, while part two is directed to priests and other liturgical planners.

Martos, Joseph. *Doors to the Sacred: A Historical Introduction to Sacraments in the Catholic Church*. Tarrytown, NY: Triumph, 1991.

Referred to several times in our text, this book is an excellent study of the history of the sacramental system and of each of the seven sacraments. Each chapter concludes with an extensive annotated bibliography, an especially helpful feature.

National Certification Standards for Professional Parish Directors of Religious Education. Washington, DC: National Conference for Catechetical Leadership, 1998.

The NCCL has developed these national certification standards to foster the appropriate initial education and formation, as well as the continuing personal and professional development, of those who serve as DREs. The standards address the various understandings and abilities needed in the personal, theological, and professional aspects of the ministry. Also included with the standards is a professional code of ethics for professional catechetical leaders.

Second Vatican Council. *Constitution on the Sacred Liturgy (Sacrosanctum Concilium)*, 1963. In Flannery, Austin, O.P., ed. *Vatican Council II, Volume I:*

The Conciliar and Postconciliar Documents. Northport, NY: Costello Publishg company, 1975. Revised edition, 1998.

    The first document promulgated by the Second Vatican Council, the *SC* is the "charter" for all subsequent efforts in the renewal of the liturgical and sacramental life of the Church.

Turner, Paul. *Confirmation: The Baby in Solomon's Court*. New York: Paulist, 1993.

    This work discusses seven models or understandings of Confirmation in use today in Catholic and Protestant churches. The historical development of each model is provided, as well as a commentary on the current practice and concerns associated with the practice.

Wagner, Nick. *MODERN LITURGY Answers the 101 Most-asked Questions about Liturgy*. San Jose: Resource Publications, Inc., 1996.

    The title describes the book exactly. Wagner's selection of questions is broad and includes queries posed about liturgical documentation, the Eucharist and the other sacraments, ministers, and certain practices. The standard question-and-answer format contributes to this being a quick and easy read.

Wilde, James A., ed. *Confirmed as Children, Affirmed as Teens: The Order of Initiation*. Font and Table Series. Chicago: Liturgy Training Publications, 1990.

    Ten authors address the "hard questions" that surround the theology and pastoral practice of Confirmation when this sacrament is celebrated prior to First Communion. "How do you celebrate sacramentally the events of youth?" is the basic question they try to answer catechetically, ecumenically, liturgically, and pastorally.

— . *When Should We Confirm? : The Order of Initiation*. Font and Table Series. Chicago: Liturgy Training Publications, 1989.

    This book discusses how the restored order of initiation in the Church (Baptism, Confirmation, and Eucharist) is not only expected but possible. Reports on the experiences of several U.S. dioceses are included.